The Man who Came Down The Attic Stairs™

Published by
ARCHAIA™

The Man who Came

Down the Attic Stairs ™

CELINE LOUP

Archaia
Los Angeles, California

Special thanks to **Sean T. Collins, Julia Gfrörer,** and **Gretchen Felker-Martin,** who have taught me so much about art and without whom this book wouldn't exist.

Cover by **Celine Loup**

Designer **Jillian Crab** with **Chelsea Roberts**
Assistant Editor **Amanda LaFranco**
Editor **Sierra Hahn**

Ross Richie CEO & Founder
Joy Huffman CFO
Matt Gagnon Editor-in-Chief
Filip Sablik President, Publishing & Marketing
Stephen Christy President, Development
Lance Kreiter Vice President, Licensing & Merchandising
Arune Singh Vice President, Marketing
Bryce Carlson Vice President, Editorial & Creative Strategy
Scott Newman Manager, Production Design
Kate Henning Manager, Operations
Spencer Simpson Manager, Sales
Sierra Hahn Executive Editor
Jeanine Schaefer Executive Editor
Dafna Pleban Senior Editor
Shannon Watters Senior Editor
Eric Harburn Senior Editor
Chris Rosa Editor
Matthew Levine Editor
Sophie Philips-Roberts Associate Editor
Gavin Gronenthal Assistant Editor
Michael Moccio Assistant Editor

Gwen Waller Assistant Editor
Amanda LaFranco Executive Assistant
Jillian Crab Design Coordinator
Michelle Ankley Design Coordinator
Kara Leopard Production Designer
Marie Krupina Production Designer
Grace Park Production Designer
Chelsea Roberts Production Design Assistant
Samantha Knapp Production Design Assistant
José Meza Live Events Lead
Stephanie Hocutt Digital Marketing Lead
Esther Kim Marketing Coordinator
Cat O'Grady Digital Marketing Coordinator
Amanda Lawson Marketing Assistant
Holly Aitchison Digital Sales Coordinator
Morgan Perry Retail Sales Coordinator
Megan Christopher Operations Coordinator
Rodrigo Hernandez Mailroom Assistant
Zipporah Smith Operations Assistant
Breanna Sarpy Executive Assistant

THE MAN WHO CAME DOWN THE ATTIC STAIRS, **September 2019.** Published by Archaia, a division of Boom Entertainment, Inc. The Man Who Came Down the Attic Stairs is ™ & © 2019 Celine Mireille Loup. All rights reserved. Archaia™ and the Archaia logo are trademarks of Boom Entertainment, Inc., registered in various countries and categories. All characters, events, and institutions depicted herein are fictional. Any similarity between any of the names, characters, persons, events, and/or institutions in this publication to actual names, characters, and persons, whether living or dead, events, and/or institutions is unintended and purely coincidental.

BOOM! Studios, 5670 Wilshire Boulevard, Suite 400, Los Angeles, CA 90036-5679. Printed in China. First Printing.

ISBN: 978-1-68415-352-7 , eISBN: 978-1-64144-335-7

To Erik

If only Plath could have married someone like you.
Thank you with all my heart.

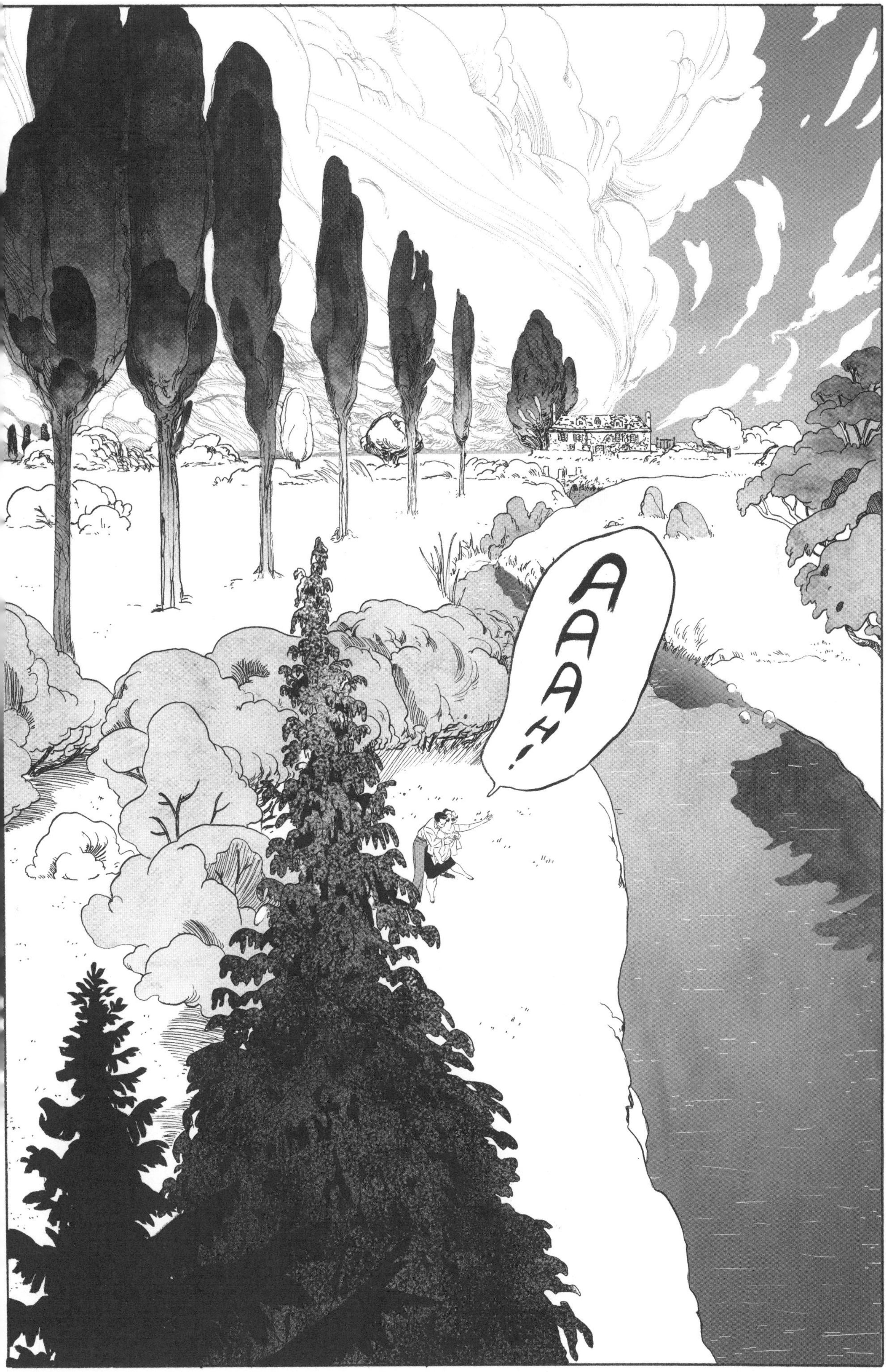
AAAAH!

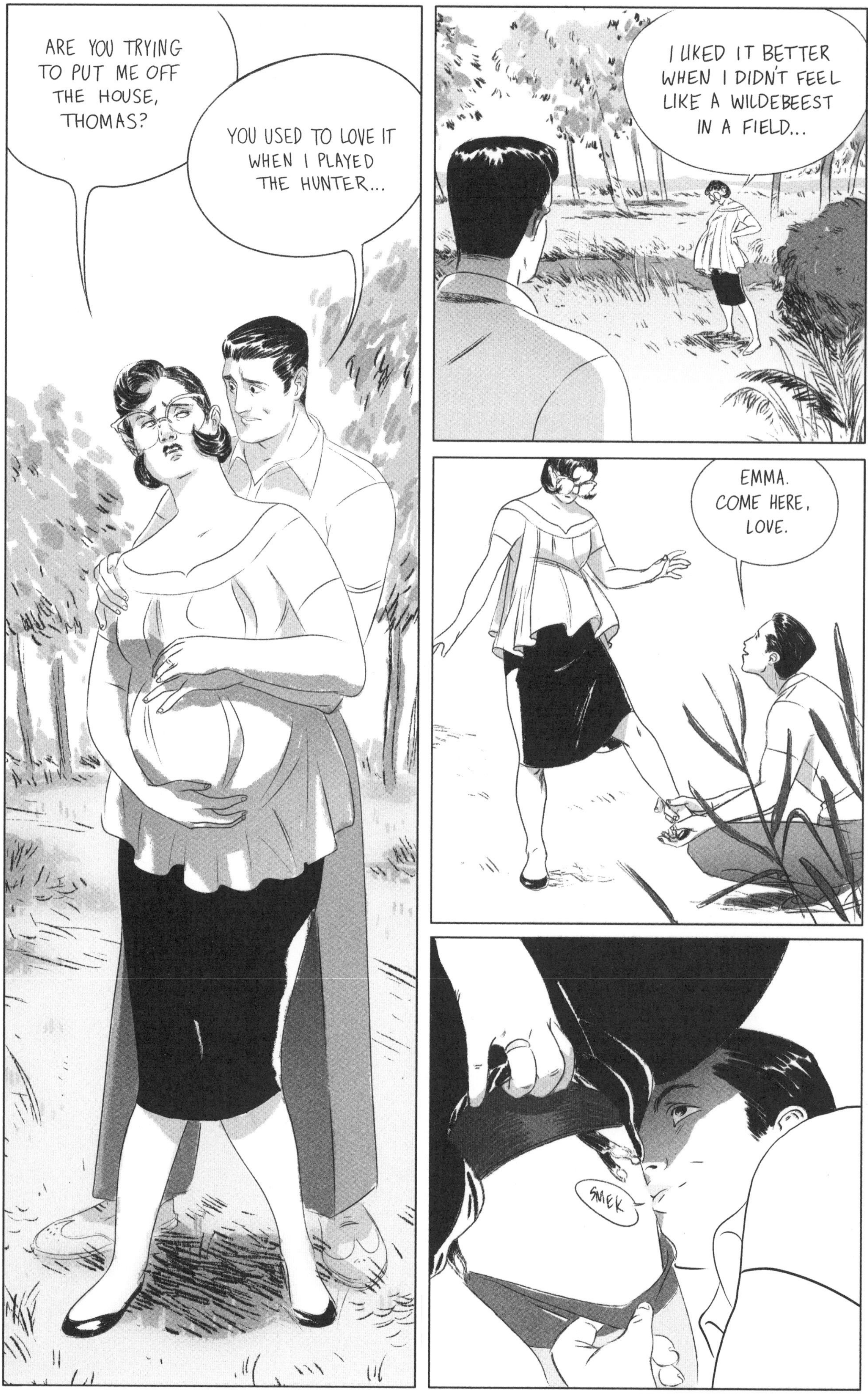
ARE YOU TRYING TO PUT ME OFF THE HOUSE, THOMAS?
YOU USED TO LOVE IT WHEN I PLAYED THE HUNTER...
I LIKED IT BETTER WHEN I DIDN'T FEEL LIKE A WILDEBEEST IN A FIELD...
EMMA. COME HERE, LOVE.
SMEK

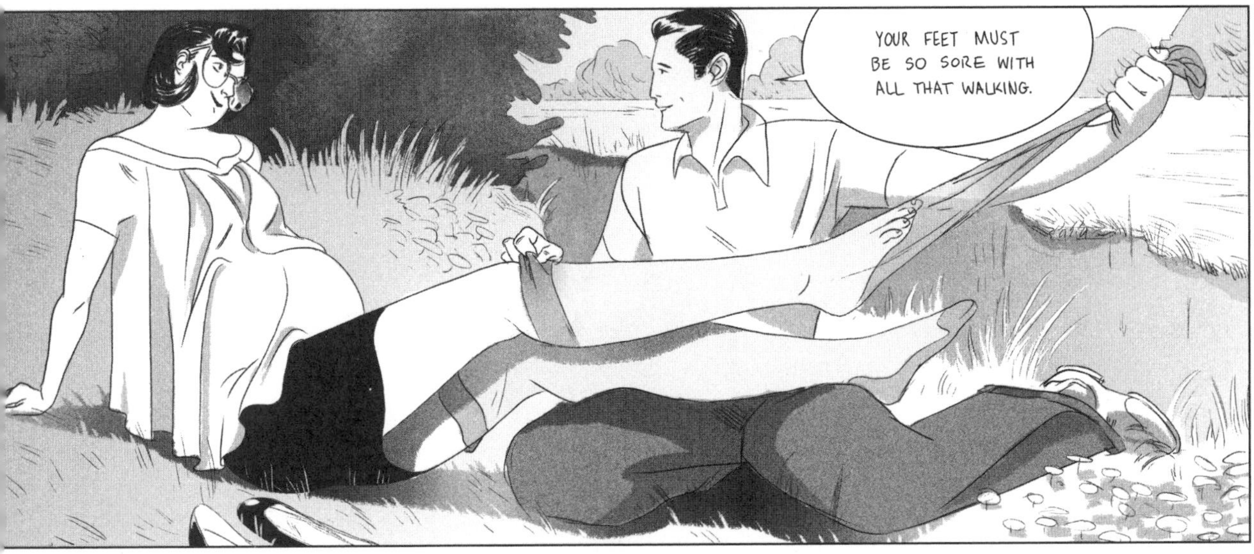
YOUR FEET MUST BE SO SORE WITH ALL THAT WALKING.

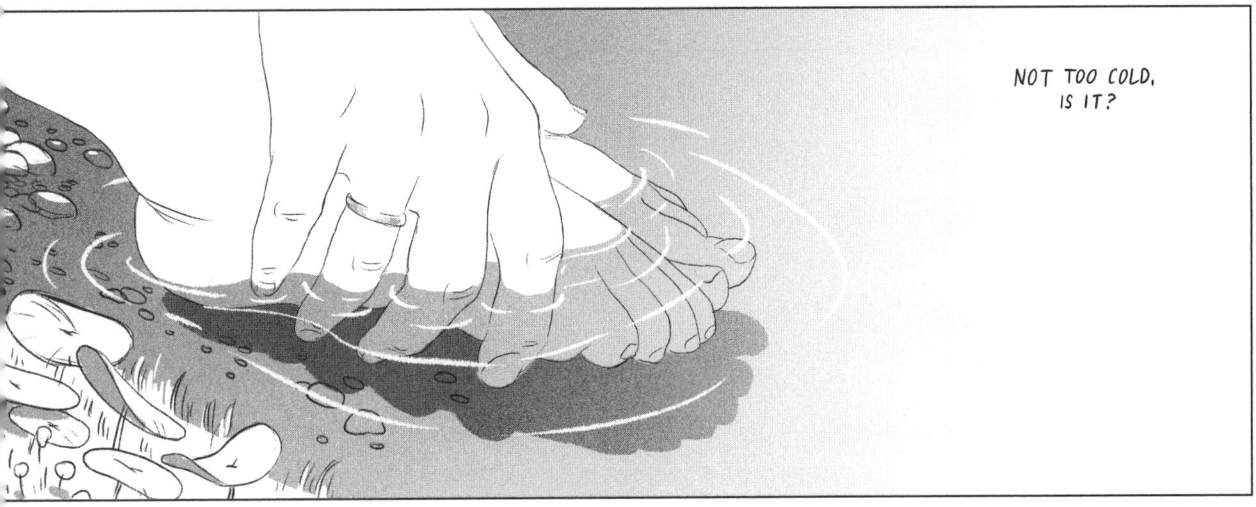
NOT TOO COLD, IS IT?

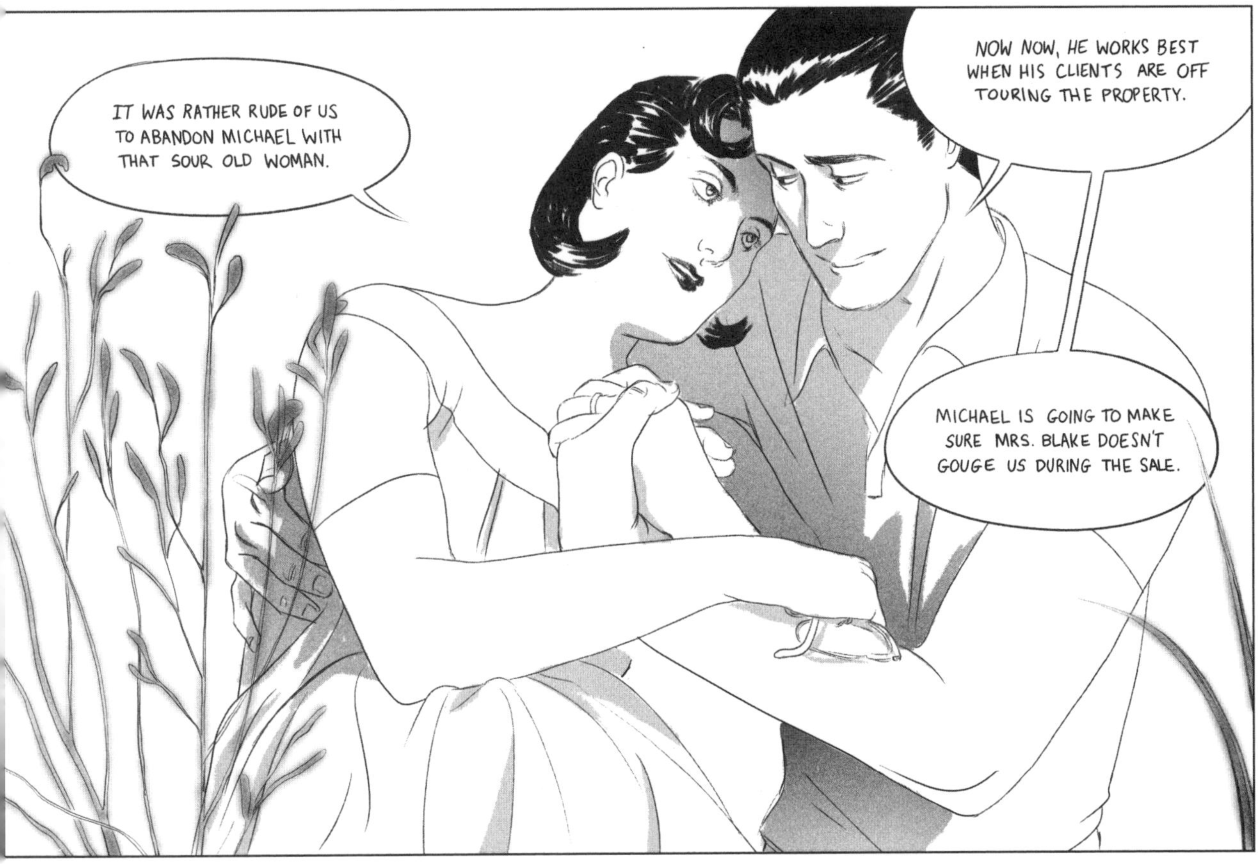
IT WAS RATHER RUDE OF US TO ABANDON MICHAEL WITH THAT SOUR OLD WOMAN.
NOW NOW, HE WORKS BEST WHEN HIS CLIENTS ARE OFF TOURING THE PROPERTY.
MICHAEL IS GOING TO MAKE SURE MRS. BLAKE DOESN'T GOUGE US DURING THE SALE.

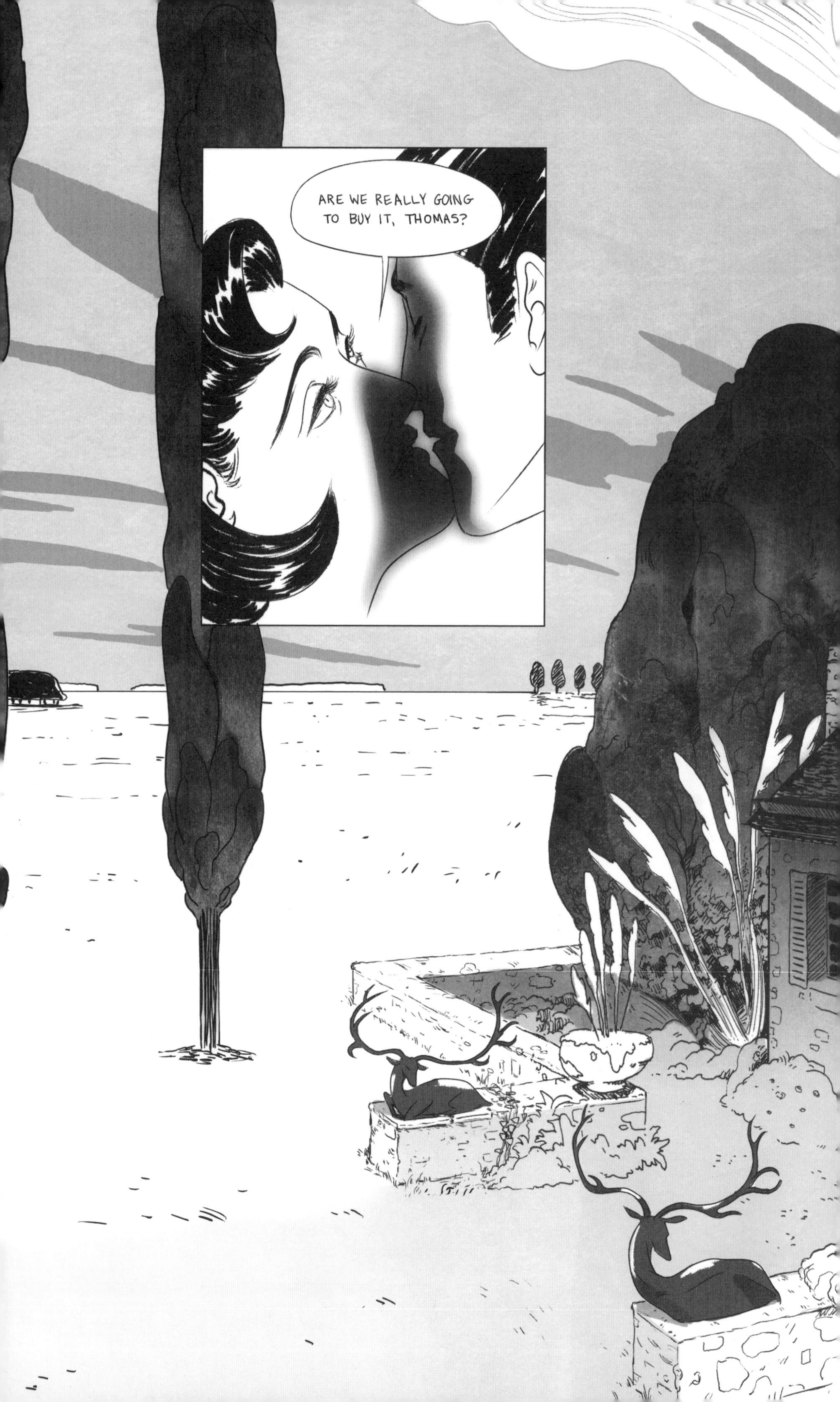
ARE WE REALLY GOING TO BUY IT, THOMAS?

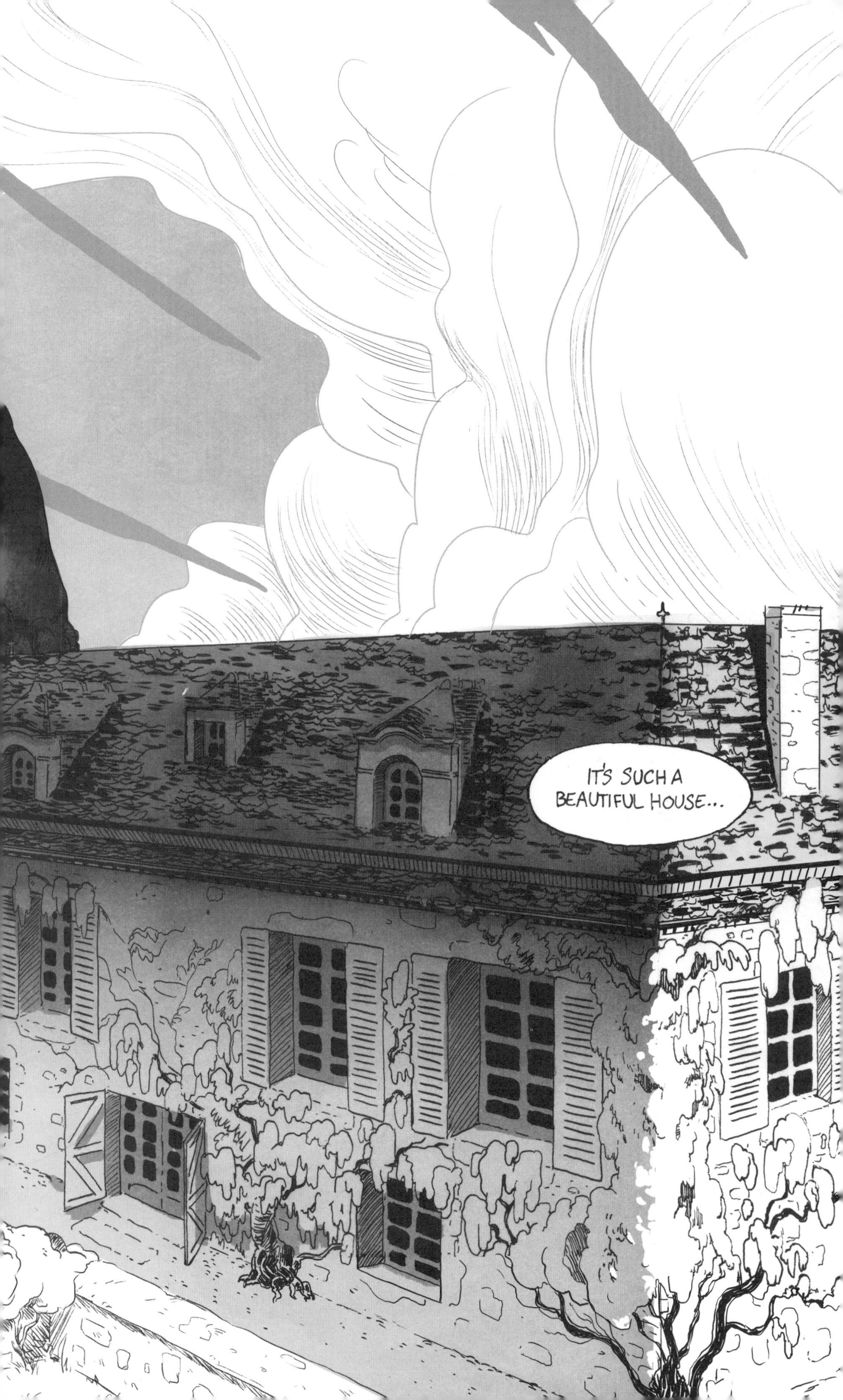
IT'S SUCH A BEAUTIFUL HOUSE...

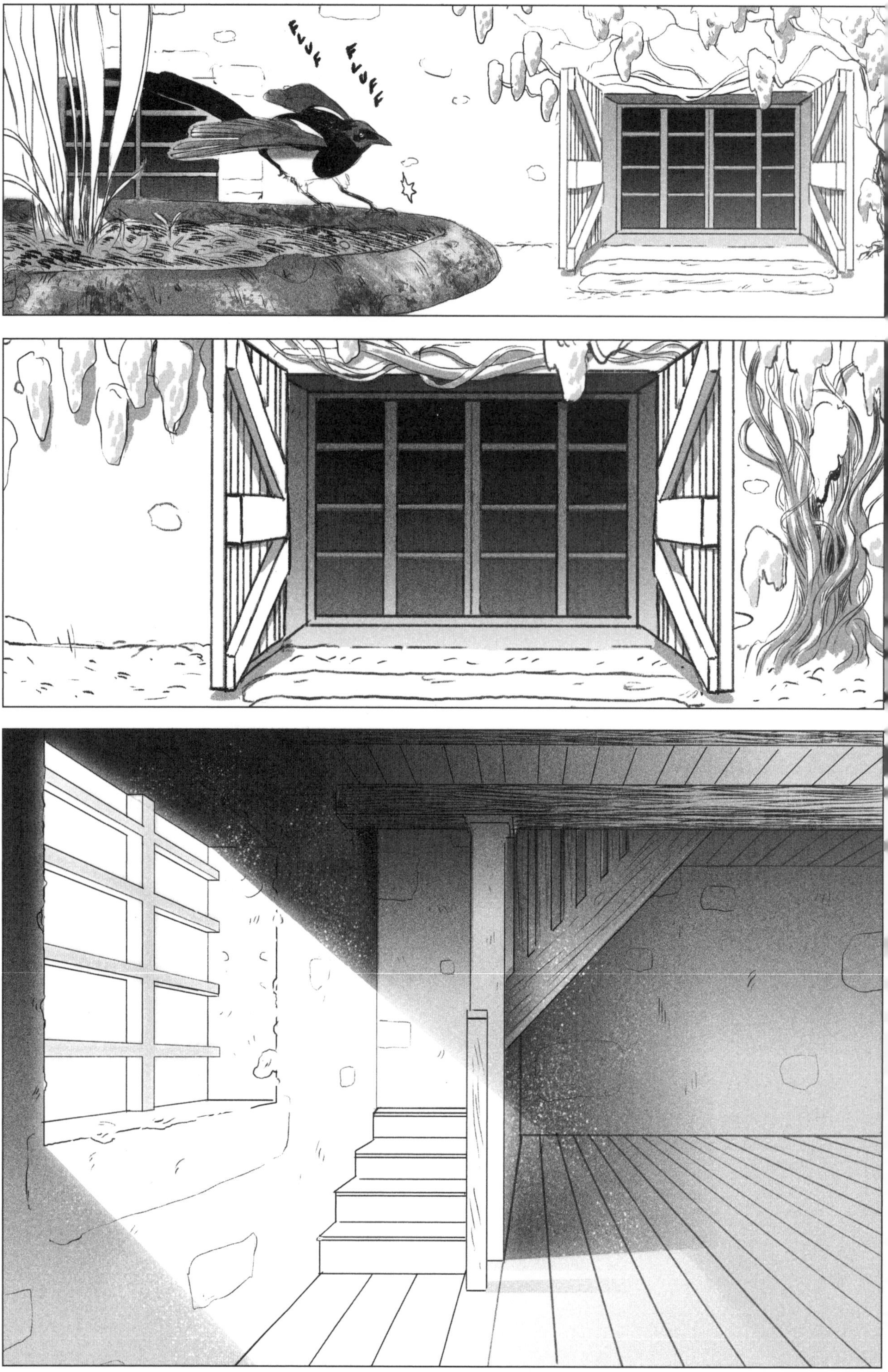
FVUF
FVUFF

PLIP
PLIP
TICK
TICK
TICK
TICK
TICK
TICK
TICK
TICK
TICK
DONG
DONG
DONG
DONG
FLAP
FLAP
FLAP

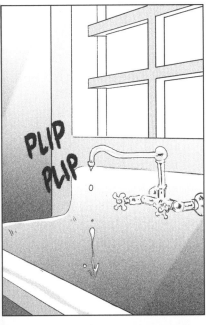

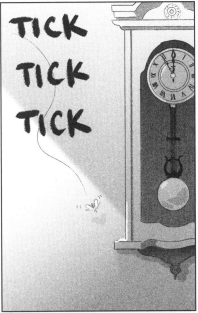

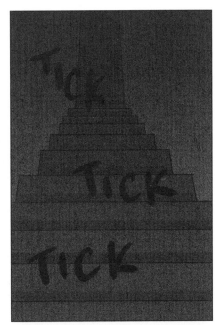

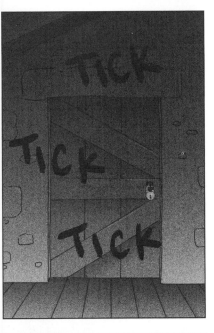

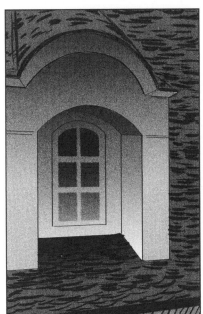

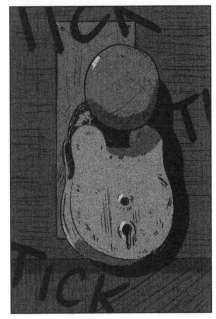

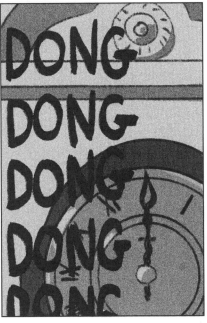

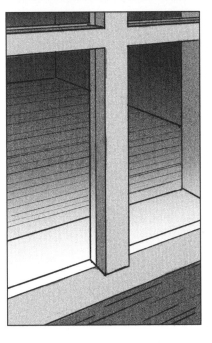

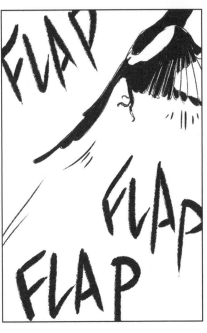

SO THOMAS BOUGHT THE HOUSE; HE BEGAN HIS WORK AT ST. JOHNS AND YOUR MARRIAGE SEEMED TO BE OFF TO A GREAT START.

WHY THEN, MRS. FLOURNOY, DO YOU BELIEVE YOUR HUSBAND SENT YOU TO SEE ME?

I DISGRACED MYSELF.

NORMALLY I DON'T AGREE TO SEE PATIENTS ON THE WEEKEND, MRS. FLOURNOY, BUT SEEING AS HOW YOUR HUSBAND HAS THE CAR DURING THE WEEK, AND AFTER ALL HIS FAMILY HAS DONE FOR ST. JOHN'S...

I'M A DANGER TO MY CHILD.

tick tick tick tick tick

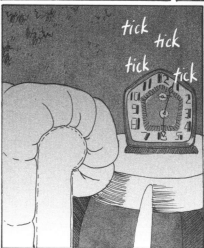

tick tick tick tick

tick tick tick tick tick

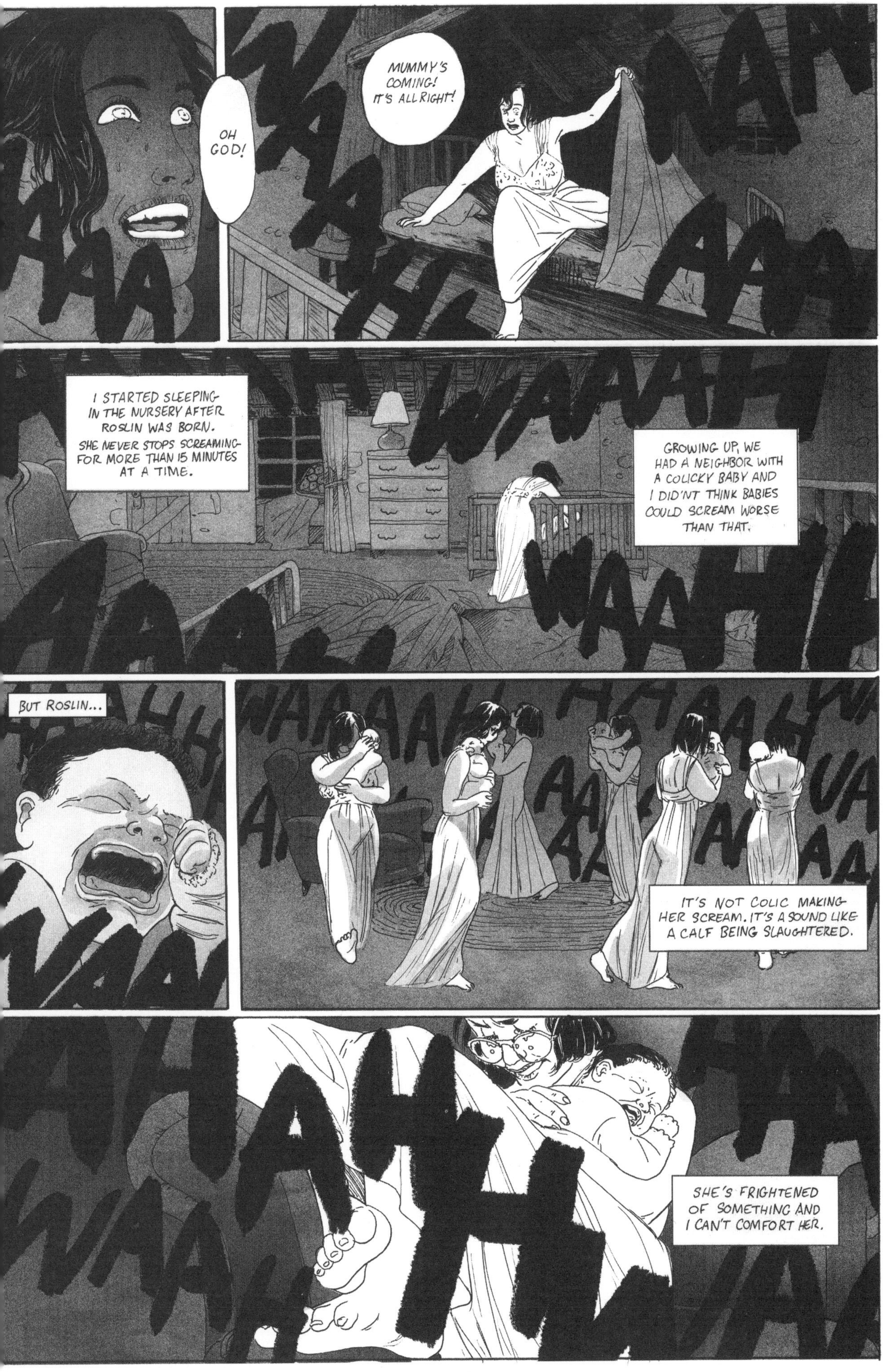

OH GOD!
MUMMY'S COMING! IT'S ALL RIGHT!
I STARTED SLEEPING IN THE NURSERY AFTER ROSLIN WAS BORN.
SHE NEVER STOPS SCREAMING FOR MORE THAN 15 MINUTES AT A TIME.
GROWING UP, WE HAD A NEIGHBOR WITH A COLICKY BABY AND I DIDN'T THINK BABIES COULD SCREAM WORSE THAN THAT.
BUT ROSLIN...
IT'S NOT COLIC MAKING HER SCREAM. IT'S A SOUND LIKE A CALF BEING SLAUGHTERED.
SHE'S FRIGHTENED OF SOMETHING AND I CAN'T COMFORT HER.

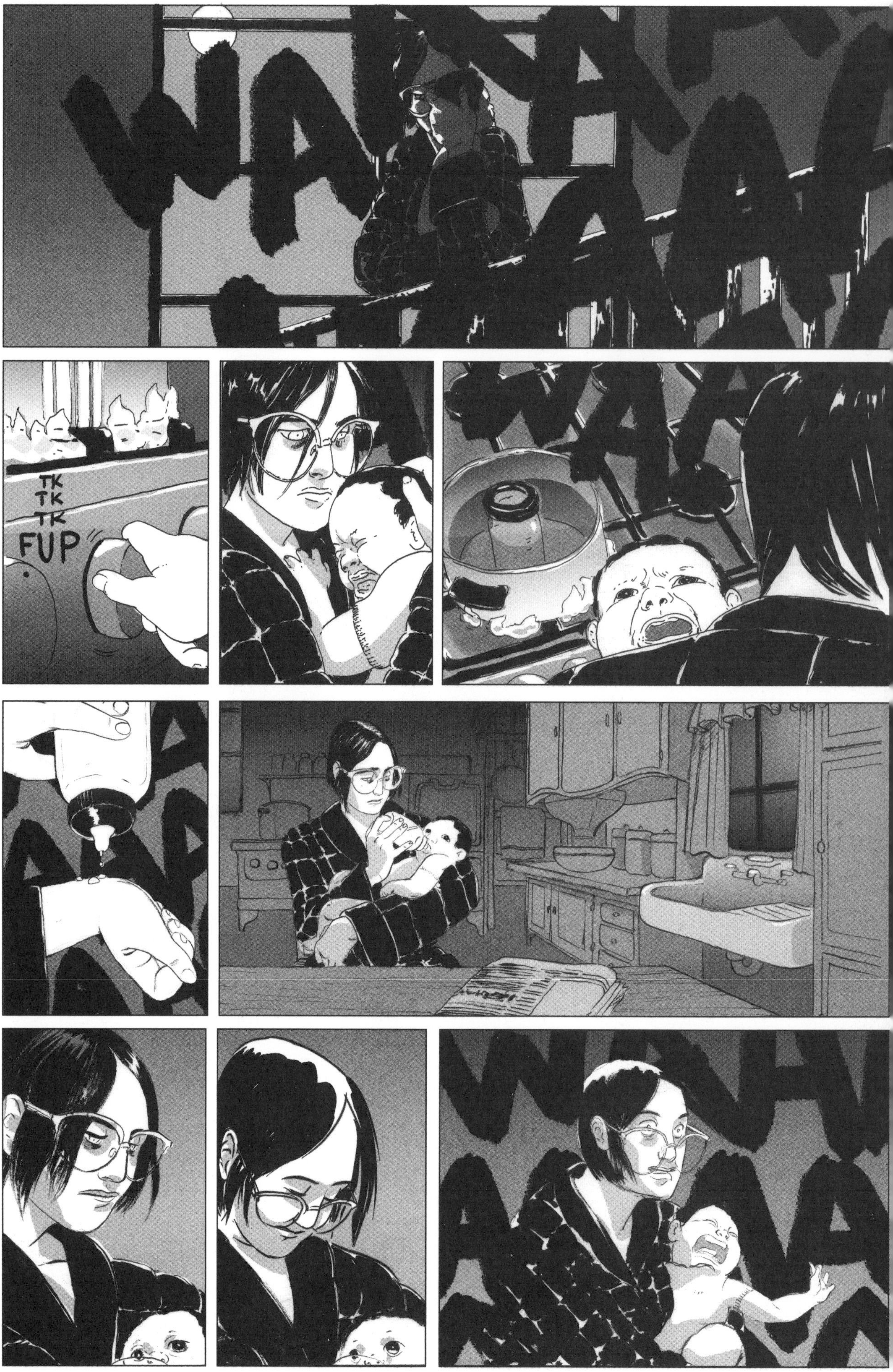
TK
TK
TK
FUP

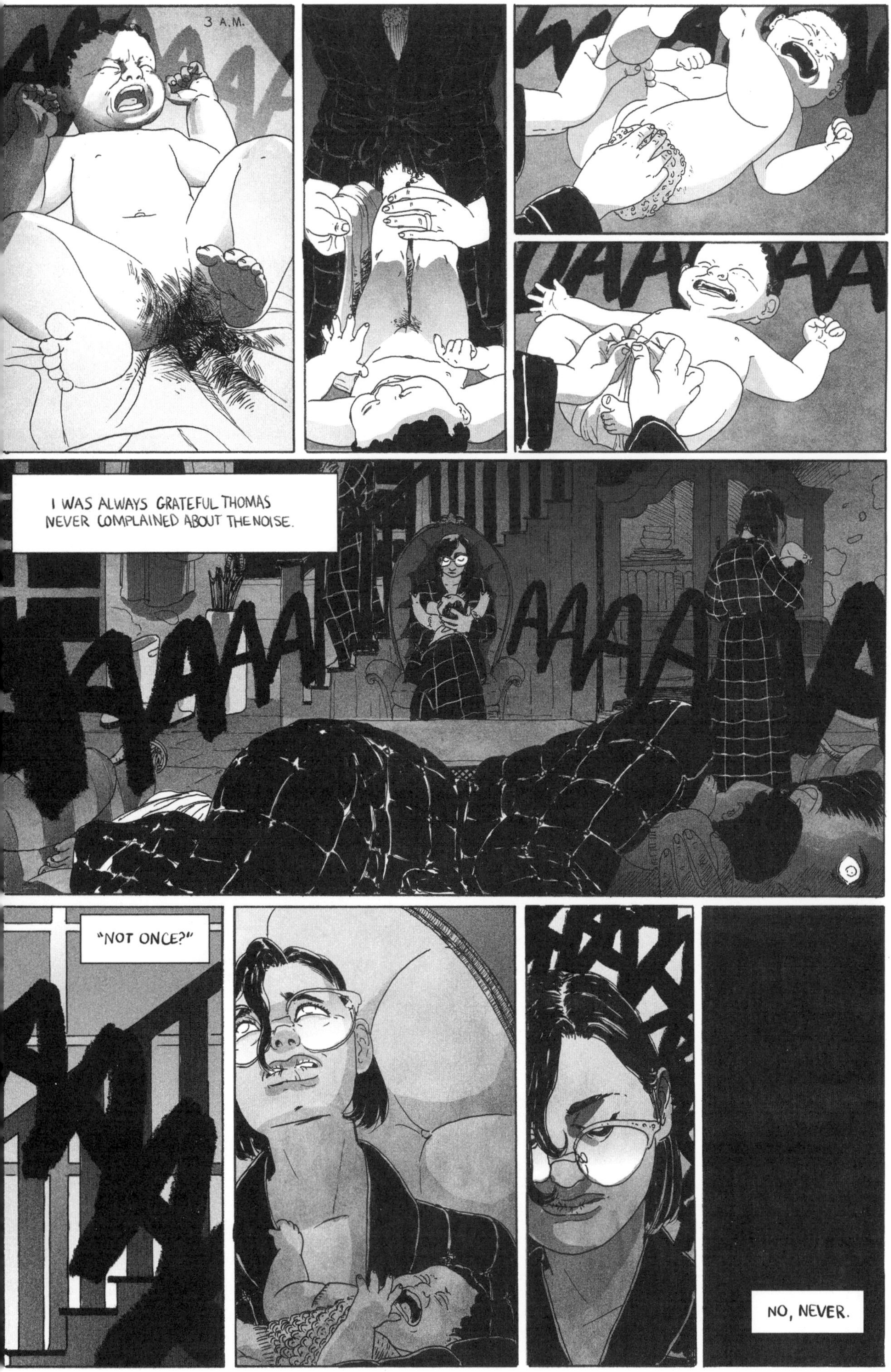
3 A.M.
I WAS ALWAYS GRATEFUL THOMAS NEVER COMPLAINED ABOUT THE NOISE.
"NOT ONCE?"
NO, NEVER.

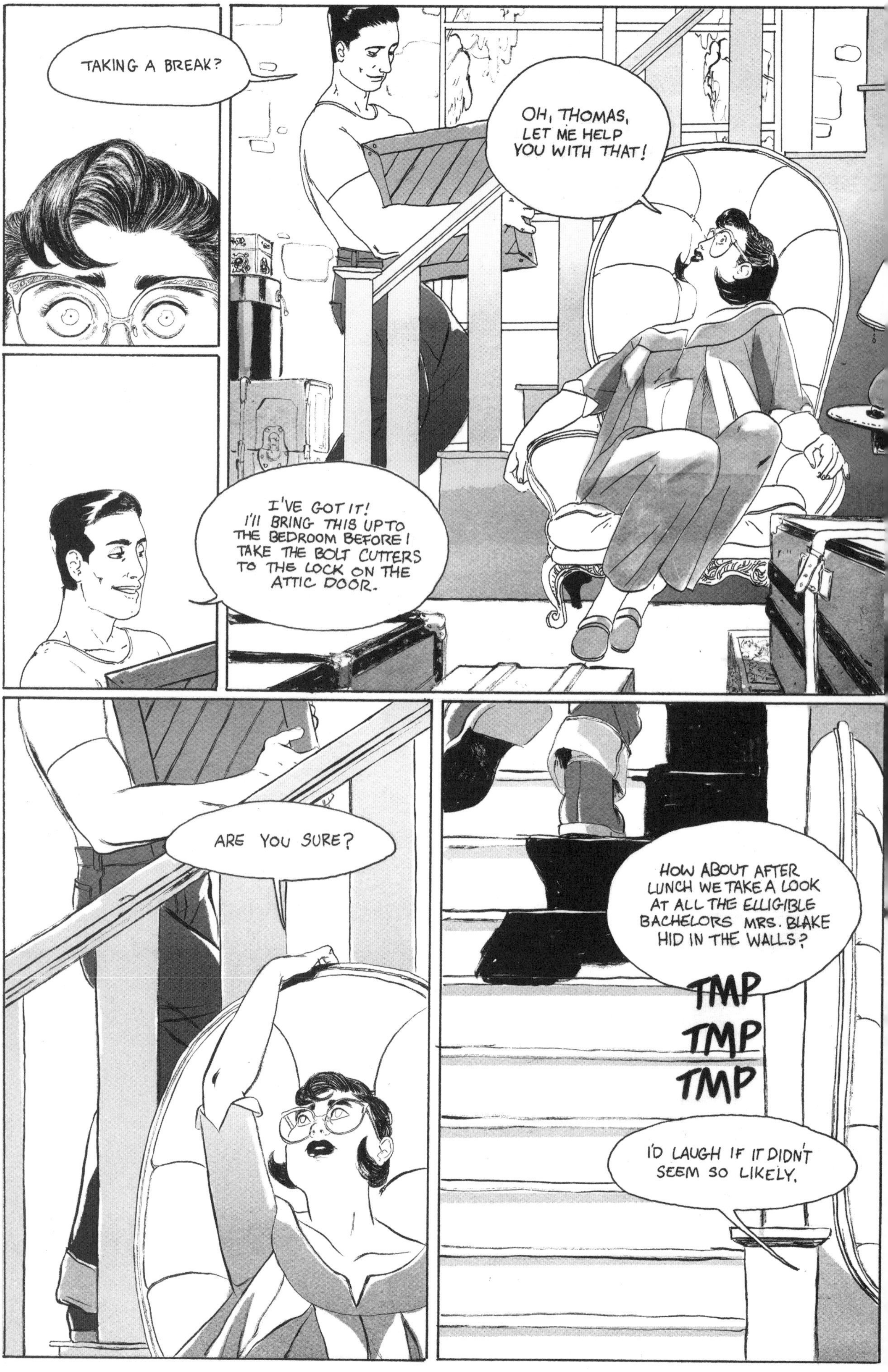
TAKING A BREAK?
OH, THOMAS, LET ME HELP YOU WITH THAT!
I'VE GOT IT! I'll BRING THIS UP TO THE BEDROOM BEFORE I TAKE THE BOLT CUTTERS TO THE LOCK ON THE ATTIC DOOR.
ARE YOU SURE?
HOW ABOUT AFTER LUNCH WE TAKE A LOOK AT ALL THE ELLIGIBLE BACHELORS MRS. BLAKE HID IN THE WALLS?
TMP
TMP
TMP
I'D LAUGH IF IT DIDN'T SEEM SO LIKELY.

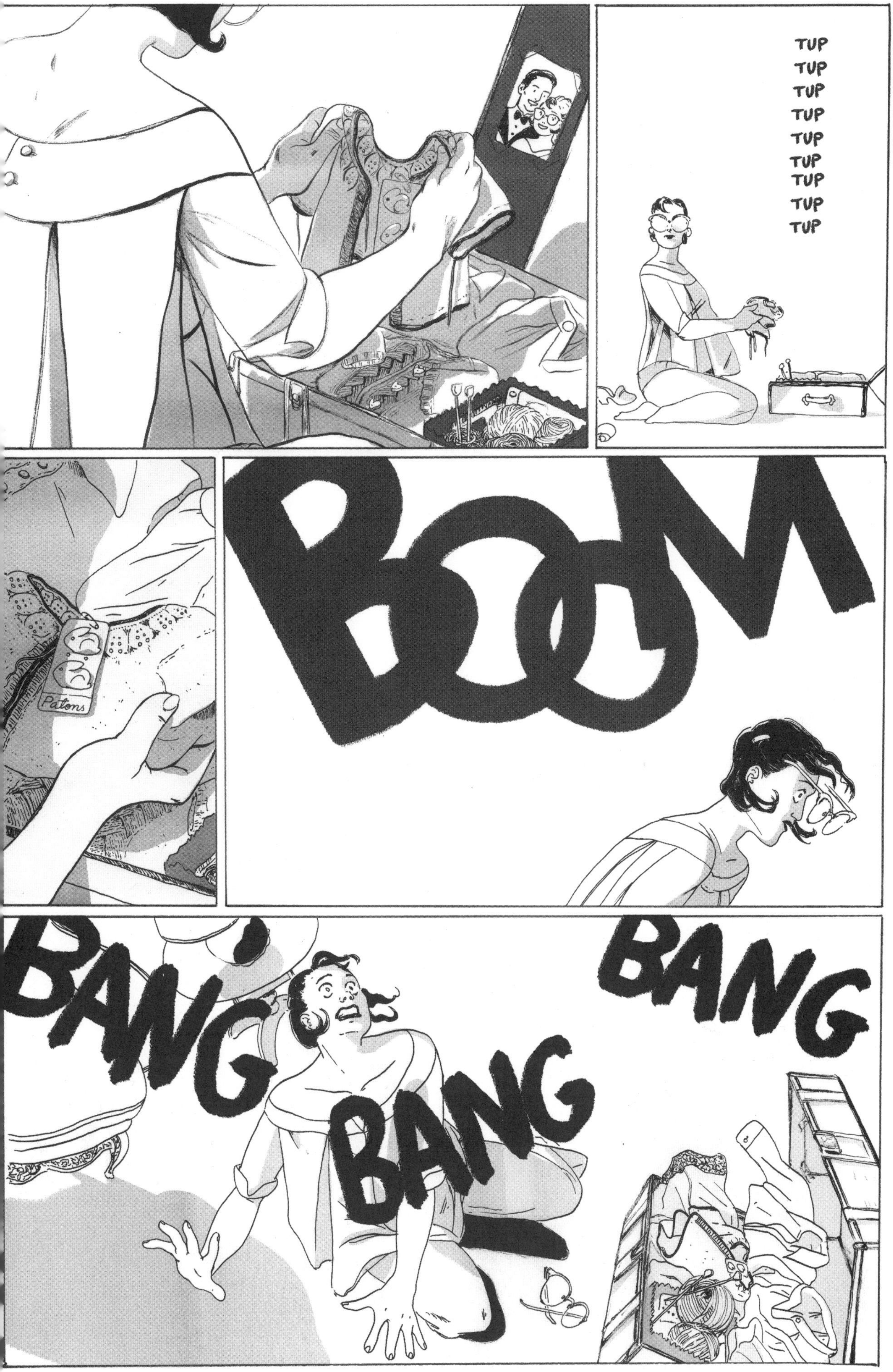
TUP
TUP
TUP
TUP
TUP
TUP
TUP
TUP
TUP
Patons
BOOM
BANG
BANG
BANG

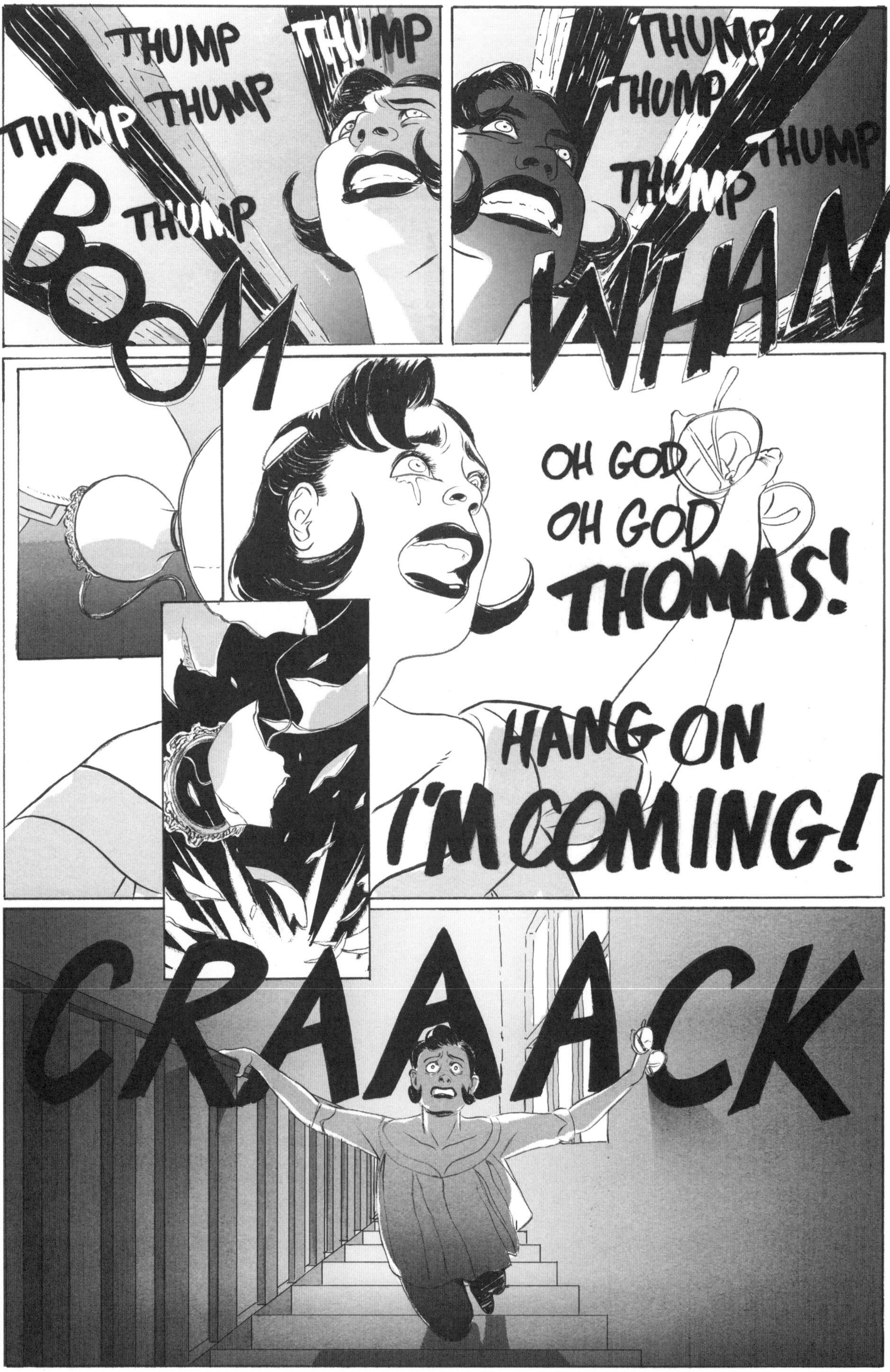
THUMP
THUMP
THUMP
THUMP
THUMP
BOOM
THUMP
THUMP
THUMP
THUMP
WHAM
OH GOD
OH GOD
THOMAS!
HANG ON
I'M COMING!
CRAAACK

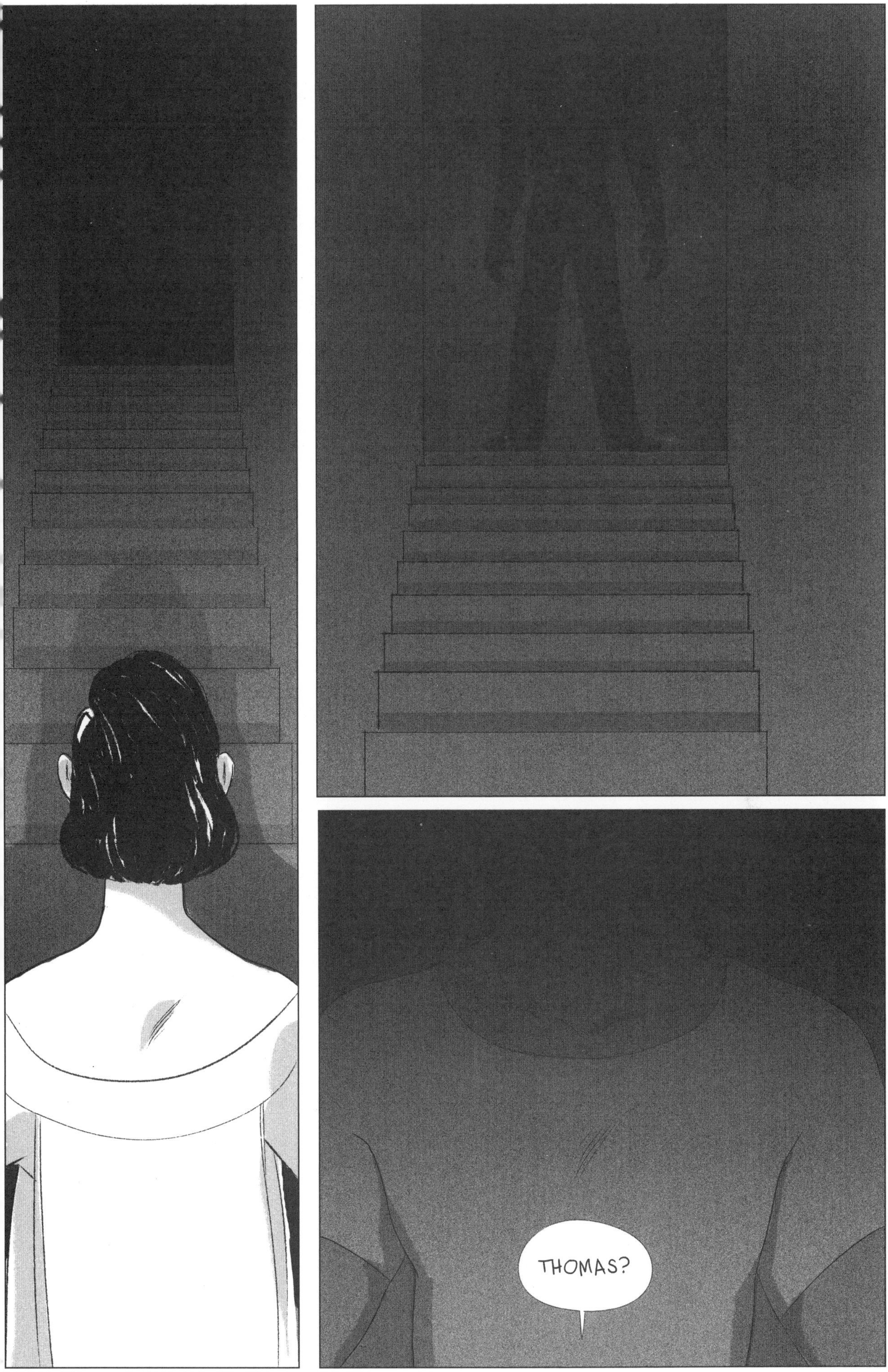
THOMAS?

TMP
THOMAS!
TMP
ARE YOU HURT AT ALL?
TMP
I WAS SO SCARED!
TMP

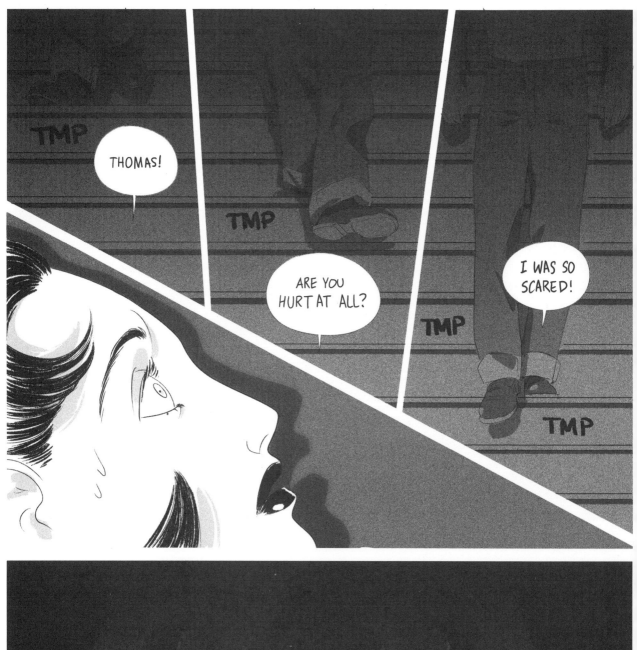

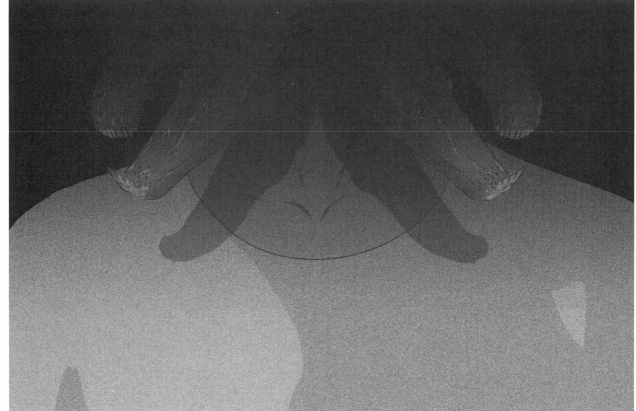

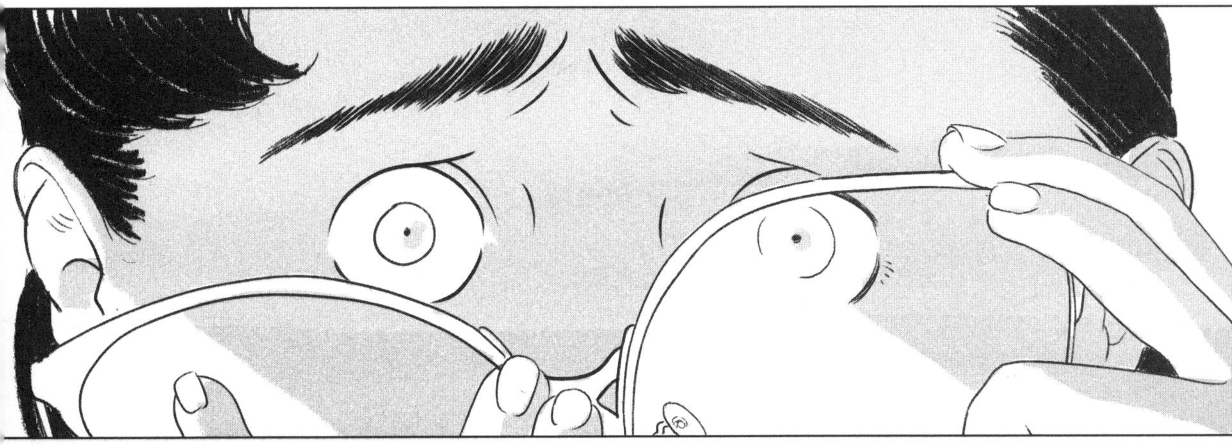

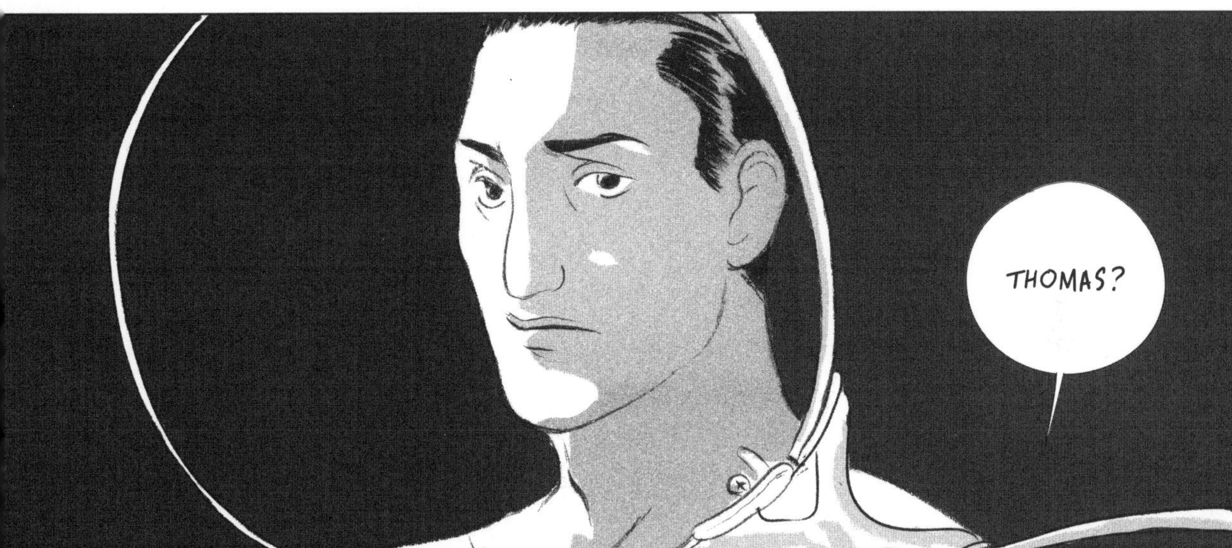
THOMAS?

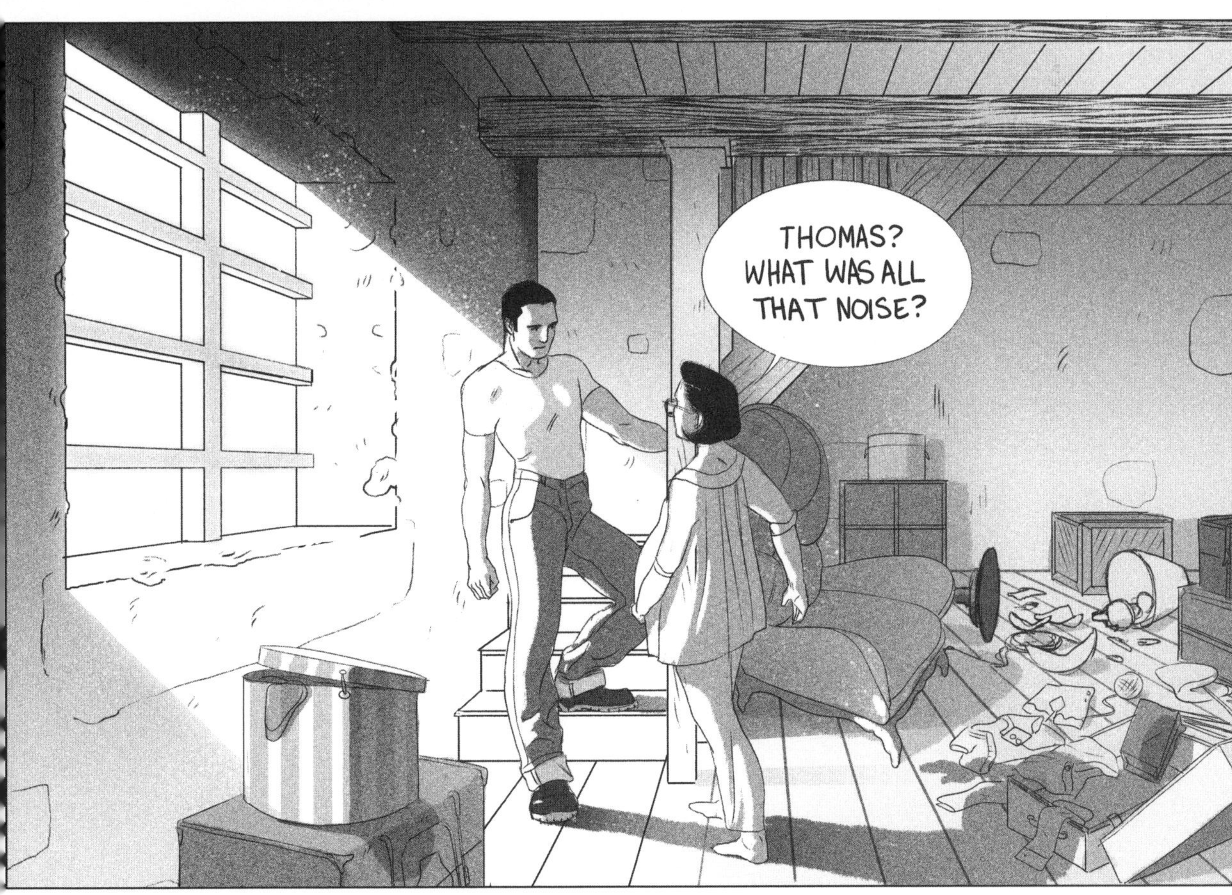
THOMAS? WHAT WAS ALL THAT NOISE?

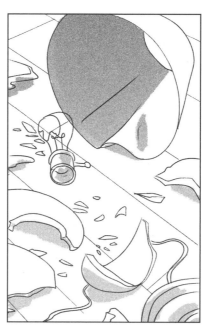

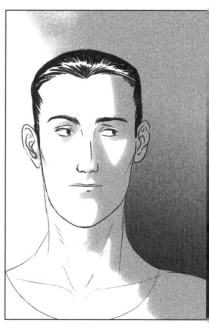

NOISE?

IT WAS DARK.
I TRIPPED OVER A
SET OF WEIGHTS.
THEY FELL OVER.

EMMA.
I TRIPPED OVER A
SET OF WEIGHTS.
THEY FELL OVER.

PLIP
PLIP
SPISH

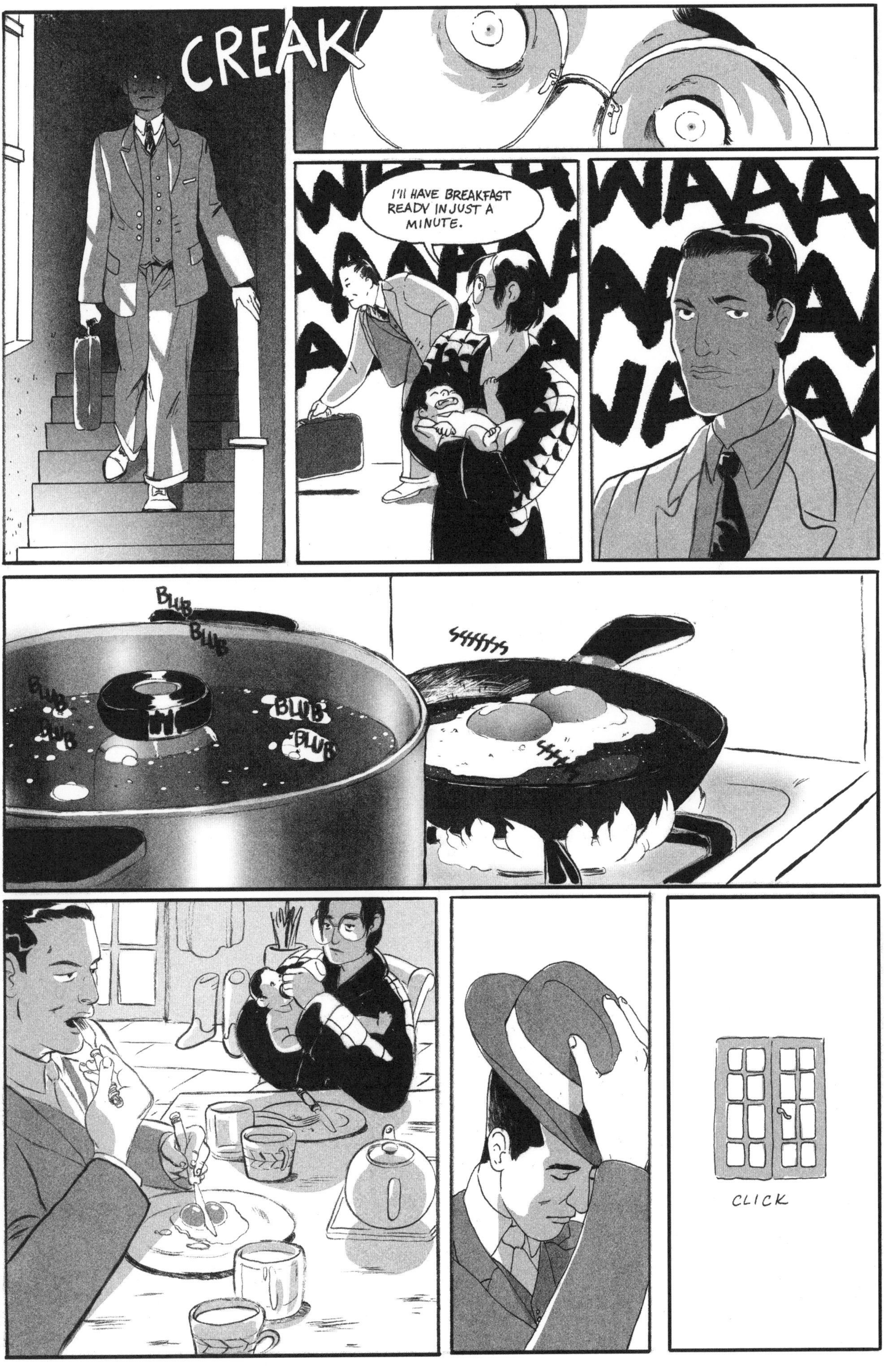
CREAK
I'll have breakfast ready in just a minute.
WAAA
BLUB
BLUB
BLUB
BLUB
BLUB
BLUB
CLICK

BLUB BLUB
BLUB BLUB BLUB
BLUB BLUB
BLUB BLUB BLUB
FWAAAAAHHH
THANK YOU FOR SEEING ME AGAIN, DR. OEMING.
CRNCH
CRNCH
CRNCH
HOW HAVE YOU BEEN SLEEPING, MRS. FLOURNOY?
CRNCH
CRNCH
I THOUGHT THINGS WOULD GET BETTER ONCE I STARTED SLEEPING IN THE ATTIC NURSERY.
CRNCH
CRNCH
CRNCH
CRNCH
CRNCH

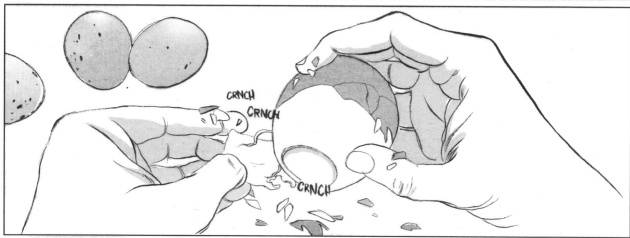

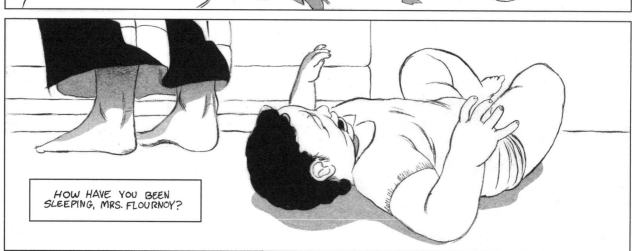

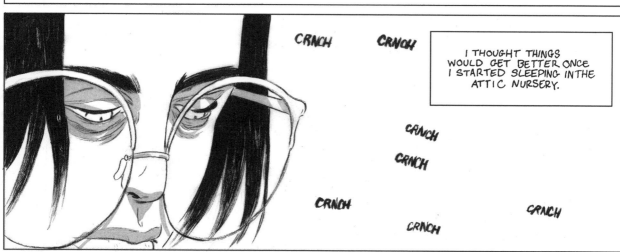

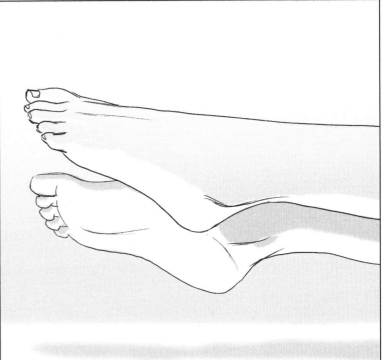

WHY DON'T YOU TRY AND HOLD HER?
YOU KNOW IT WON'T MAKE A DIFFERENCE.

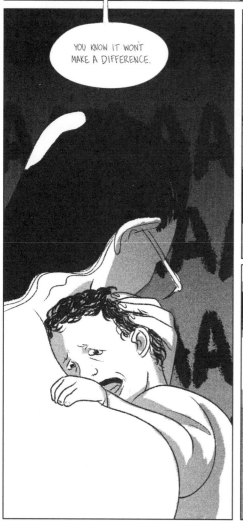

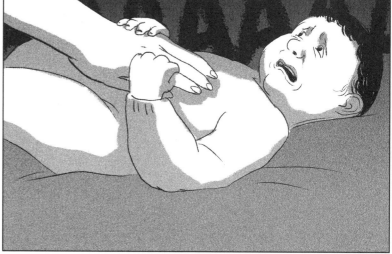

PLEASE

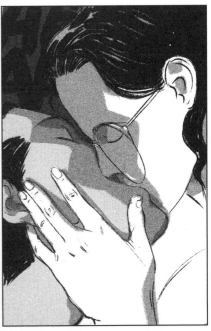

BANG BANG BANG BANG

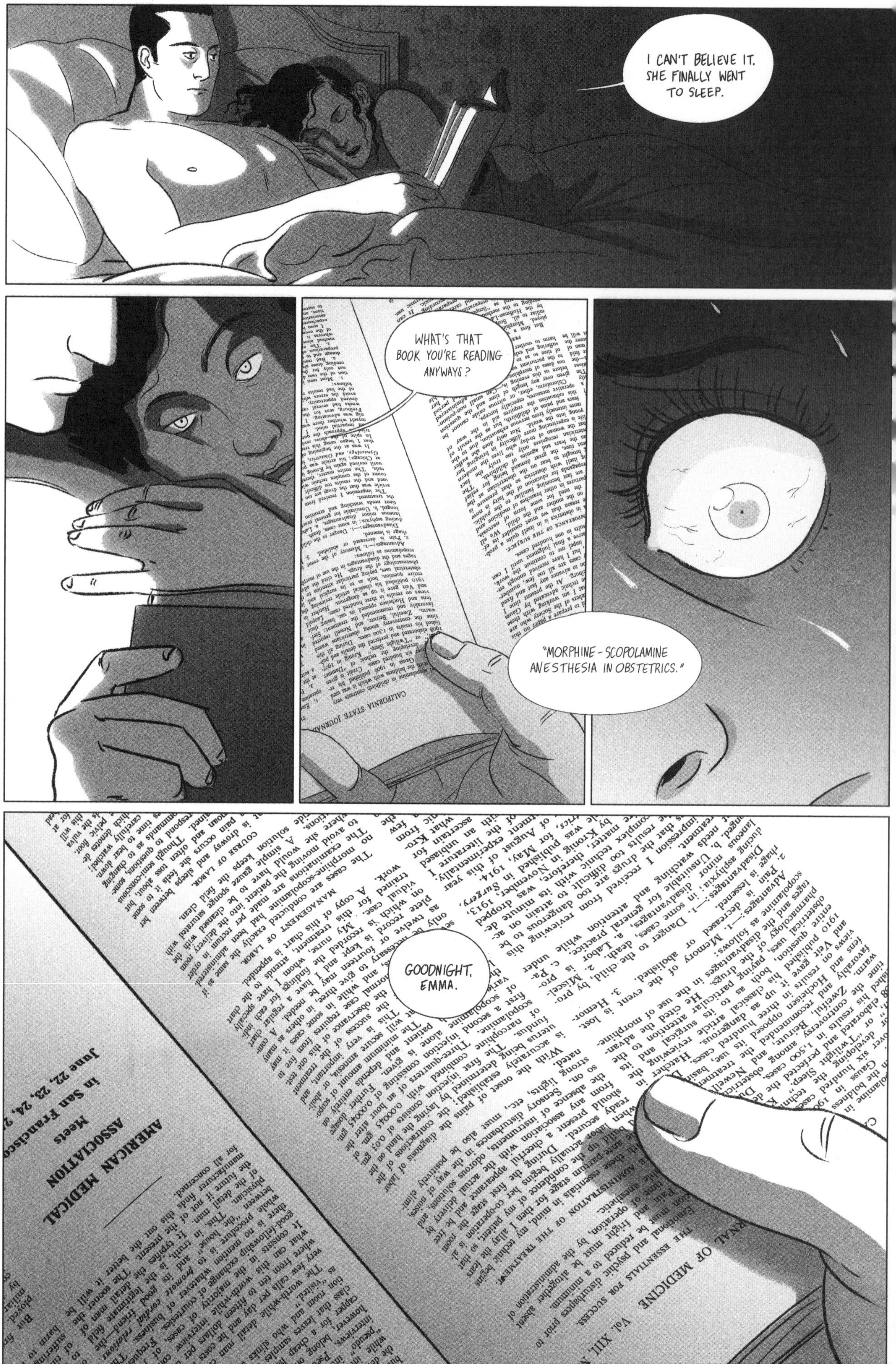
I CAN'T BELIEVE IT. SHE FINALLY WENT TO SLEEP.
WHAT'S THAT BOOK YOU'RE READING ANYWAYS?
"MORPHINE-SCOPOLAMINE ANESTHESIA IN OBSTETRICS."
GOODNIGHT, EMMA.

8 A.M.
WAAAAAAAAAAAAH
WAAAAAAAAAAA
WAAAAAAAAA
WAAAAAAAAAAAA
AAAA
FLUPAP
BLUB
BLUB
BLUB
BLUB
FSSHH

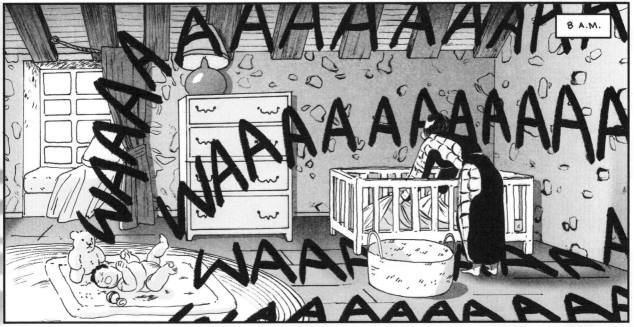

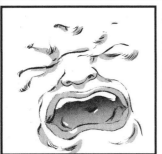

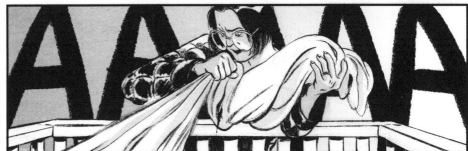

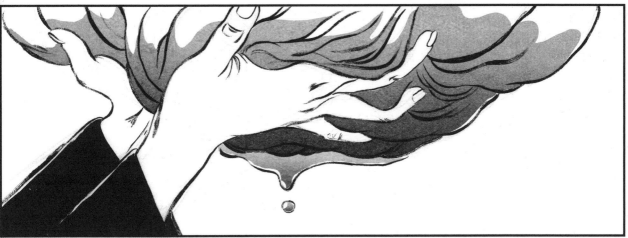

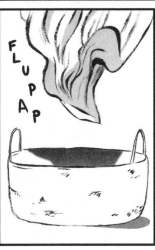

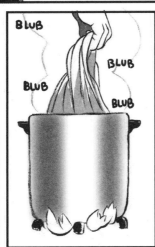

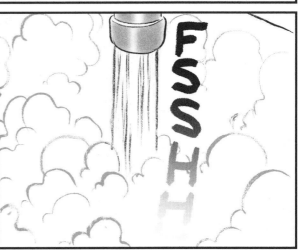

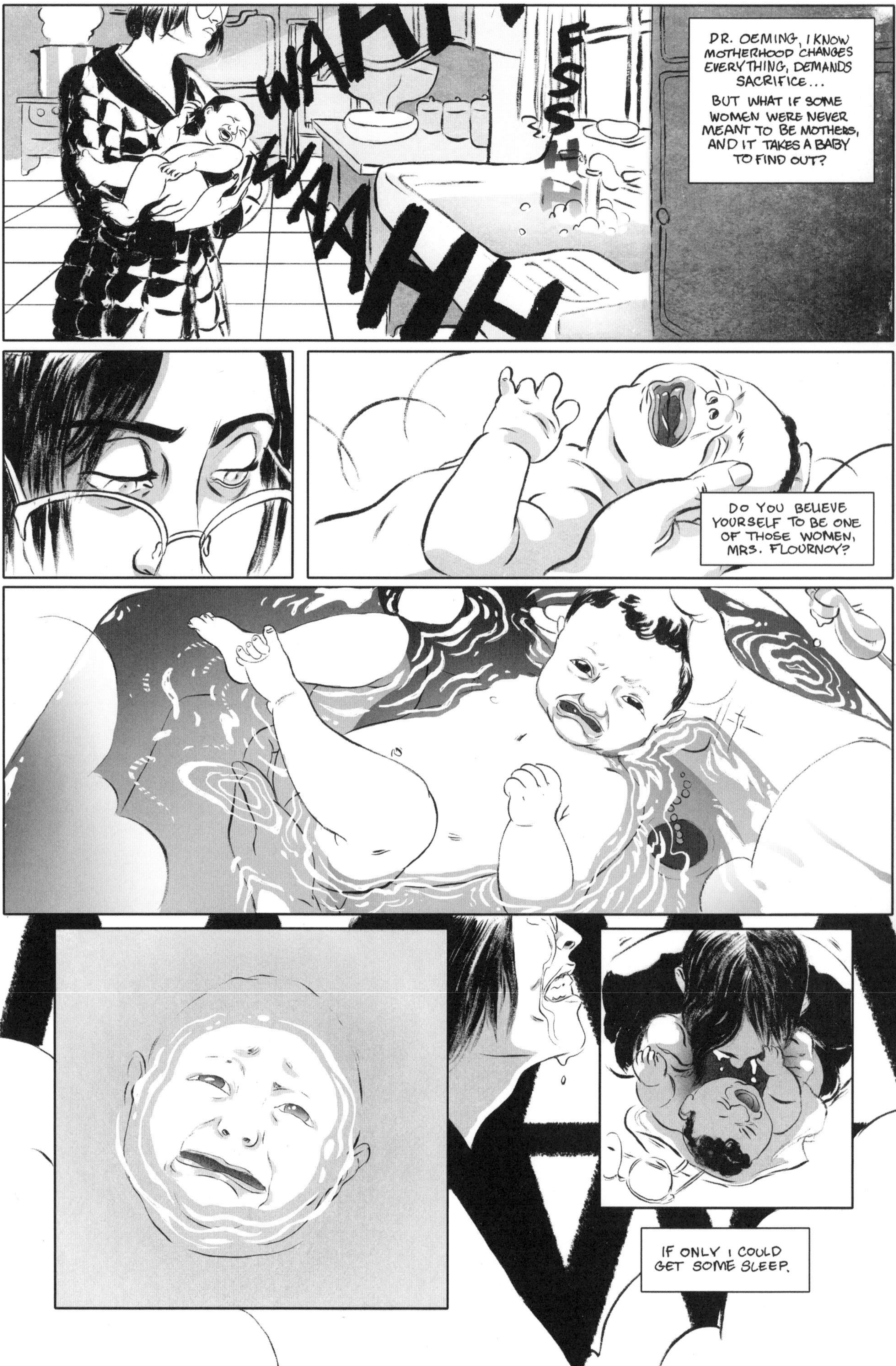
DR. OEMING, I KNOW MOTHERHOOD CHANGES EVERYTHING, DEMANDS SACRIFICE...
BUT WHAT IF SOME WOMEN WERE NEVER MEANT TO BE MOTHERS, AND IT TAKES A BABY TO FIND OUT?
WAAH!
FSSH
WAAAHH
DO YOU BELIEVE YOURSELF TO BE ONE OF THOSE WOMEN, MRS. FLOURNOY?
IF ONLY I COULD GET SOME SLEEP.

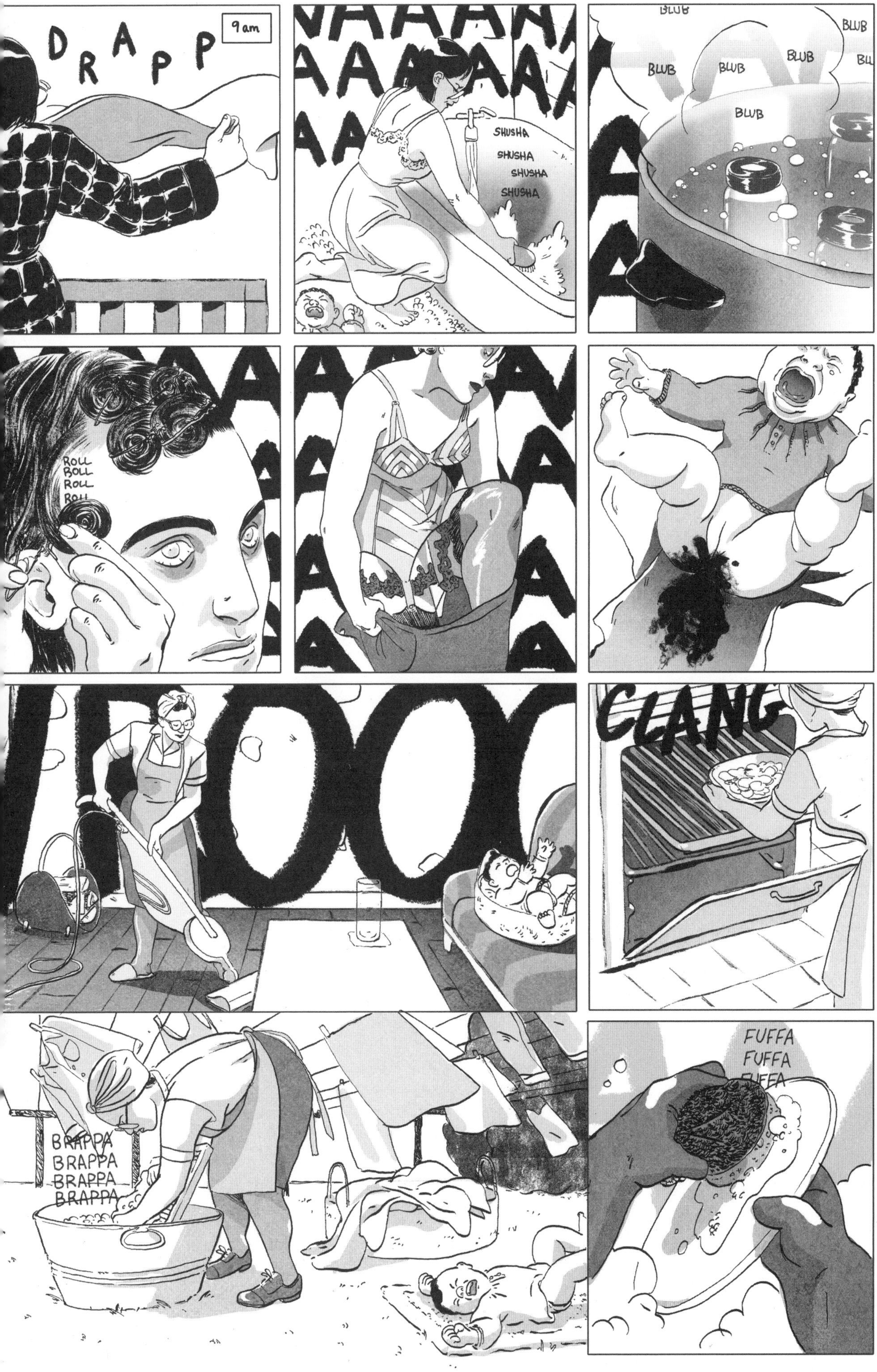
9 am
DRAPP
SHUSHA
SHUSHA
SHUSHA
SHUSHA
BLUB
BLUB
BLUB
BLUB
BLUB
BLUB
ROLL
ROLL
ROLL
CLANG
BRAPPA
BRAPPA
BRAPPA
BRAPPA
FUFFA
FUFFA

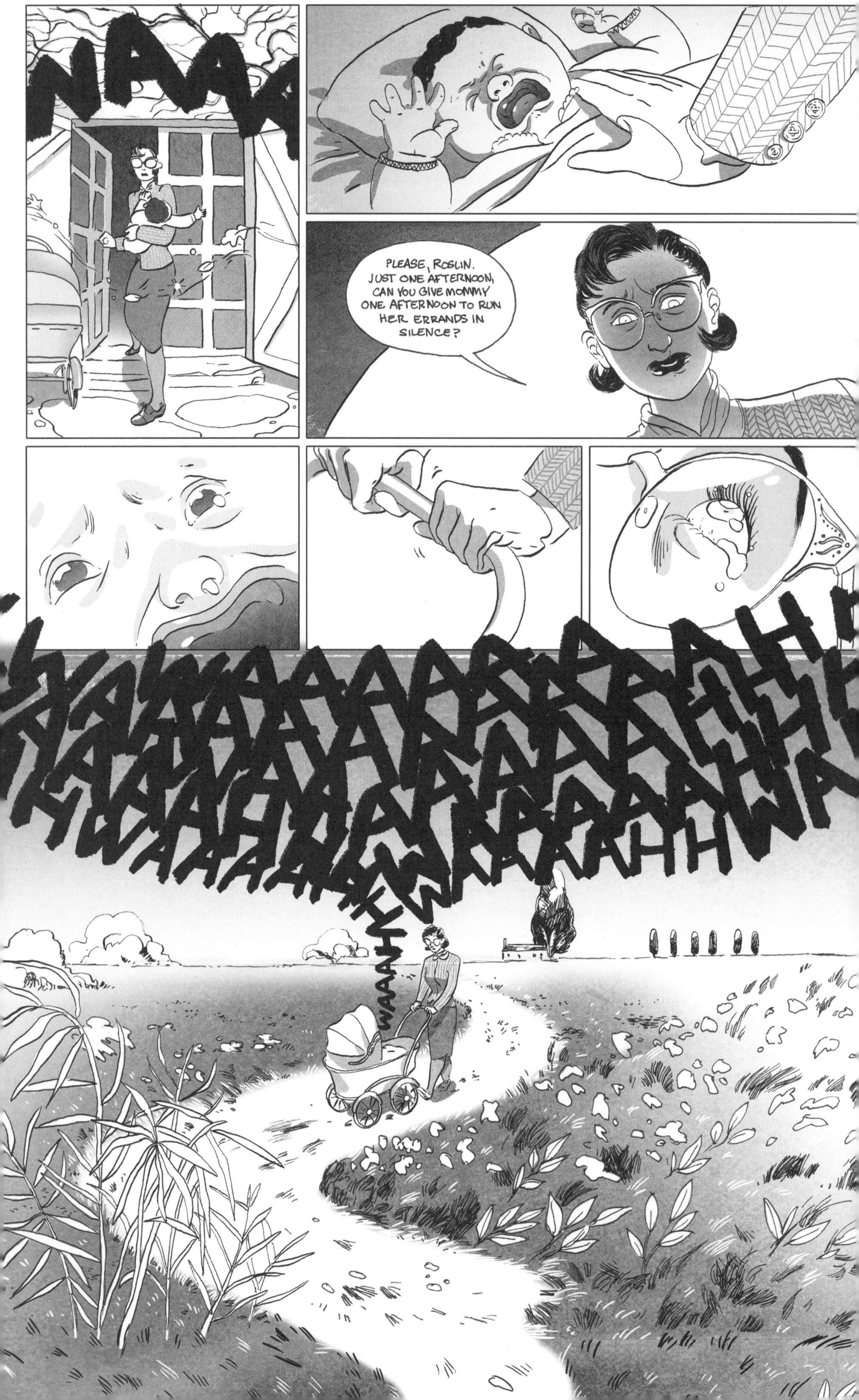
WAAA
PLEASE, ROSLIN. JUST ONE AFTERNOON, CAN YOU GIVE MOMMY ONE AFTERNOON TO RUN HER ERRANDS IN SILENCE?
WAAAAAARRRAHH
WAAAH

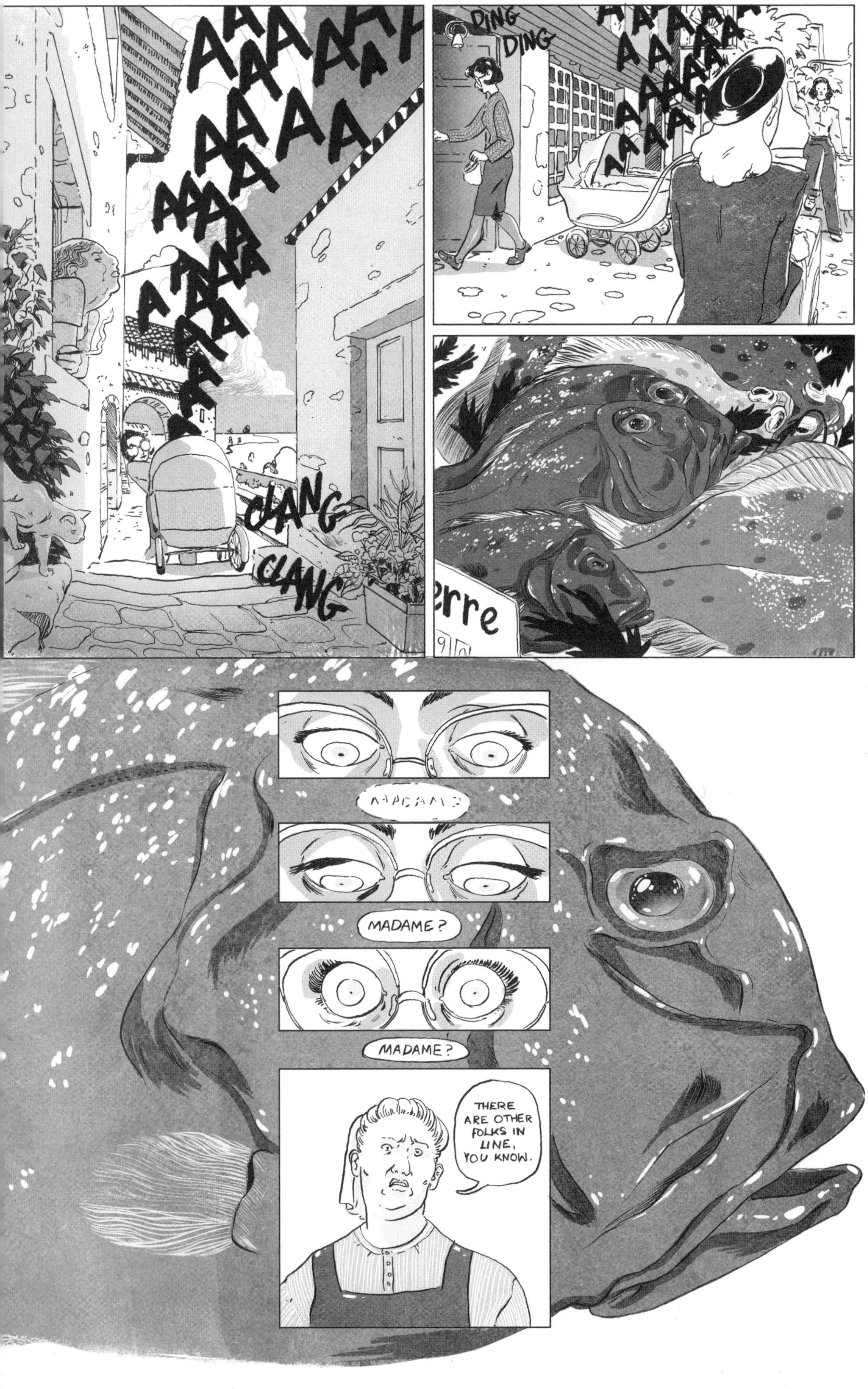
AAAAAAAAAAAAAAAAAAAAAAAA
CLANG
CLANG
DING
DING
AAAAAAAAAAAAAAAA
erre
MADAME?
MADAME?
MADAME?
THERE ARE OTHER FOLKS IN LINE, YOU KNOW.

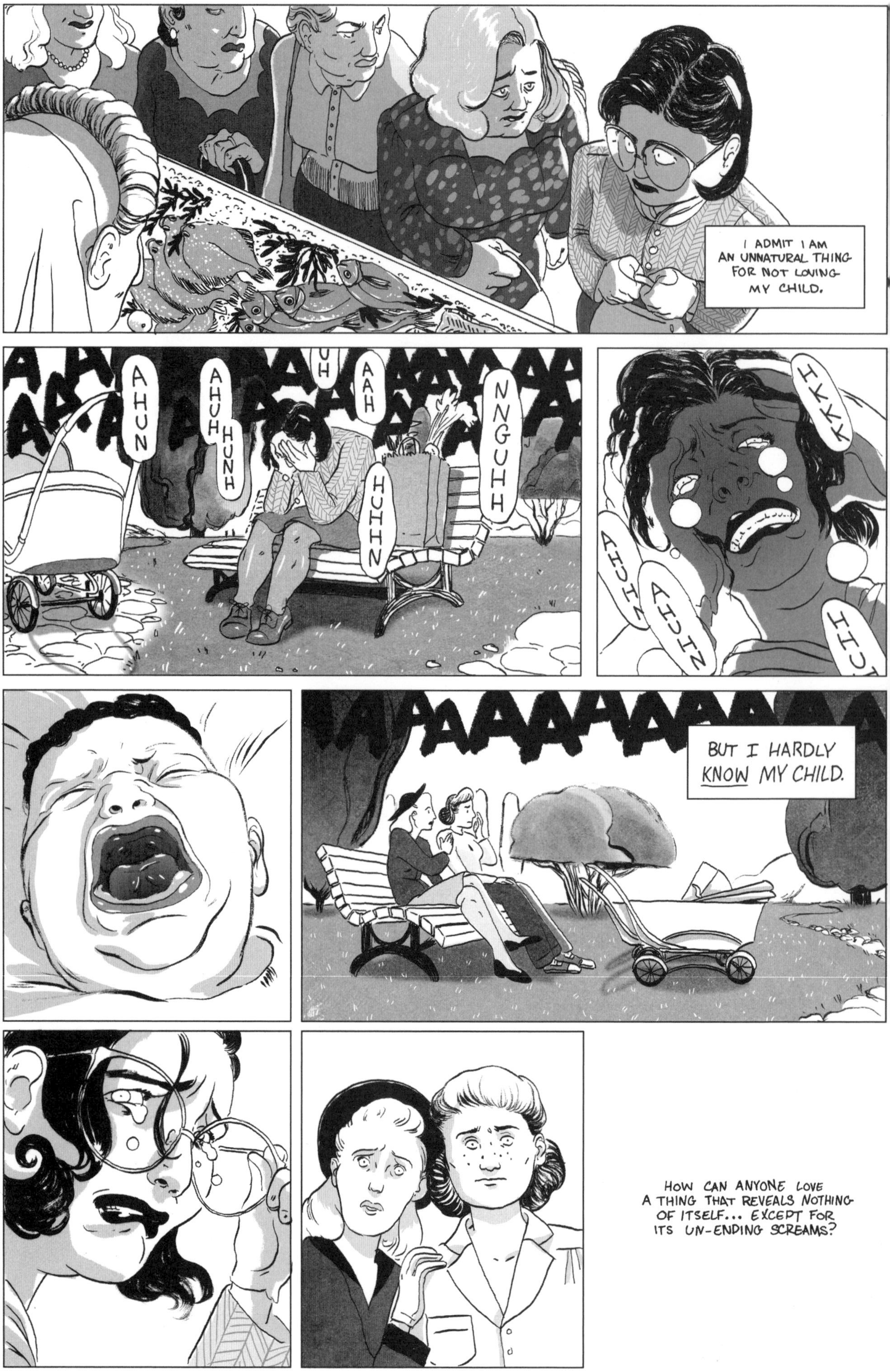

I ADMIT I AM AN UNNATURAL THING FOR NOT LOVING MY CHILD.
AHUN
AHUH
HUNH
UH
AAH
HUHHN
NNGUHH
HKKK
AHUHN
BUT I HARDLY KNOW MY CHILD.
HOW CAN ANYONE LOVE A THING THAT REVEALS NOTHING OF ITSELF... EXCEPT FOR ITS UN-ENDING SCREAMS?

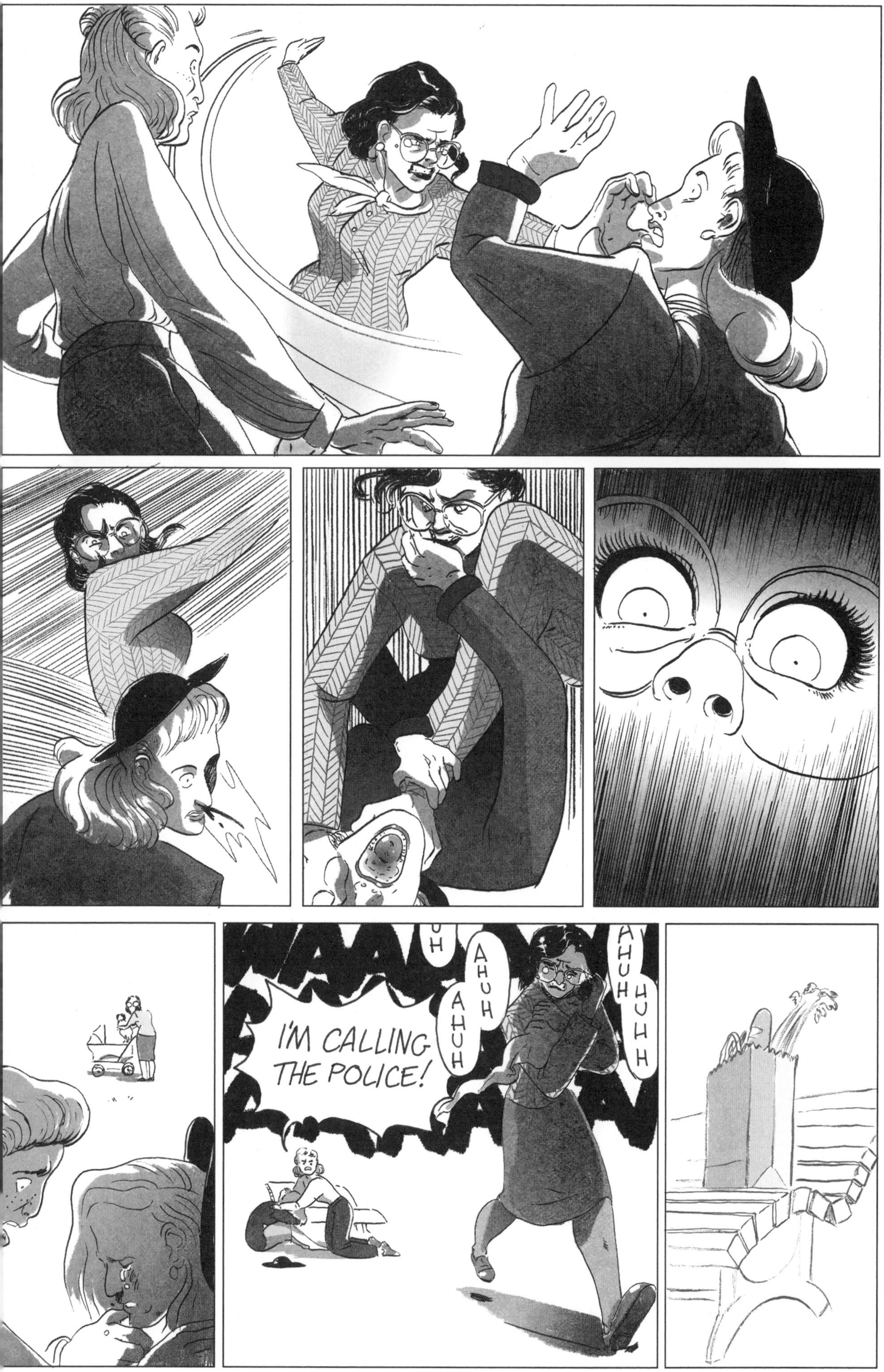
I'M CALLING THE POLICE!
UH
AHUH
AHUH
AHUH
HUHH

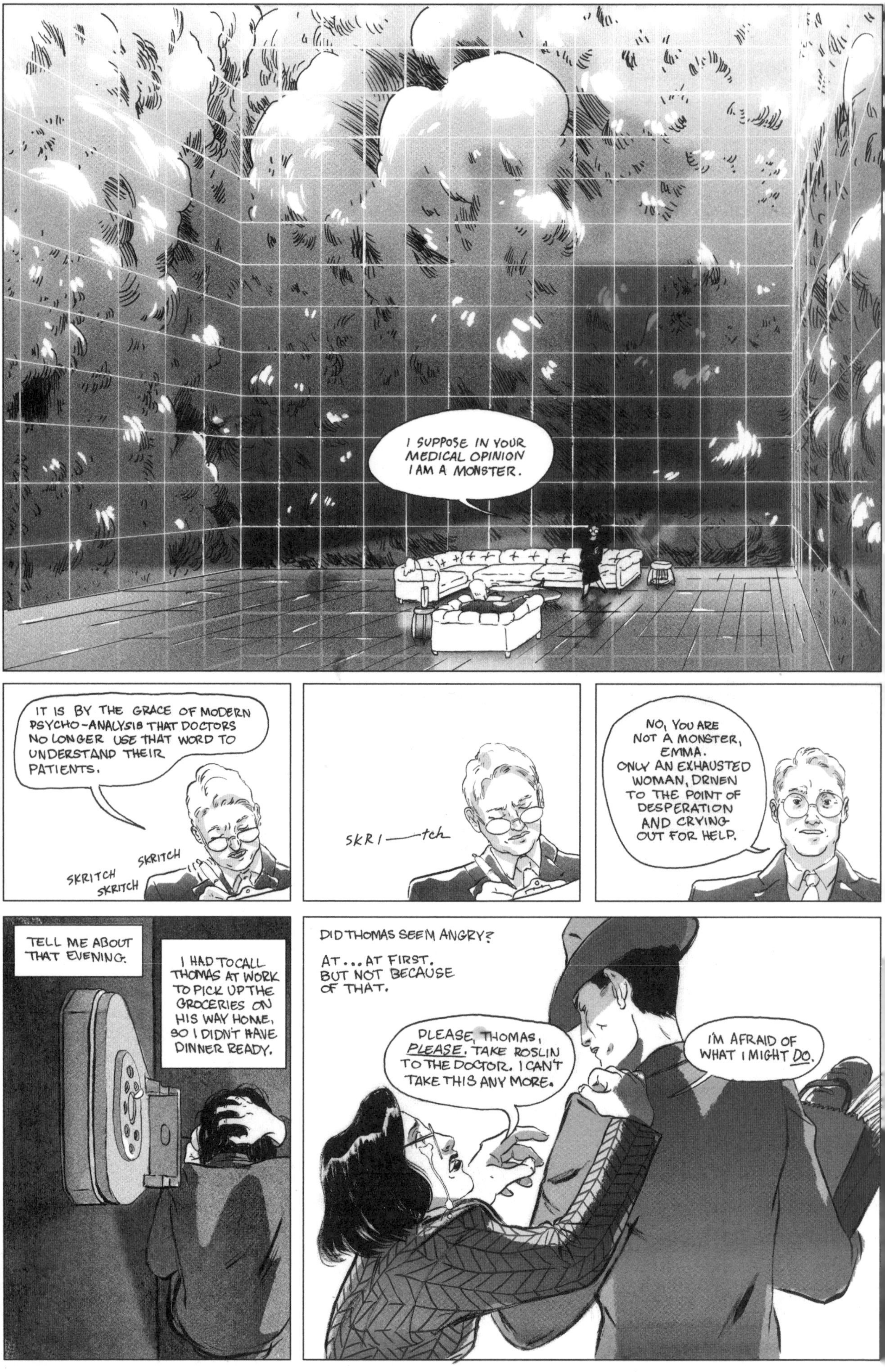
I SUPPOSE IN YOUR MEDICAL OPINION I AM A MONSTER.
IT IS BY THE GRACE OF MODERN PSYCHO-ANALYSIS THAT DOCTORS NO LONGER USE THAT WORD TO UNDERSTAND THEIR PATIENTS.
SKRITCH SKRITCH SKRITCH
SKRI——tch
NO, YOU ARE NOT A MONSTER, EMMA. ONLY AN EXHAUSTED WOMAN, DRIVEN TO THE POINT OF DESPERATION AND CRYING OUT FOR HELP.
TELL ME ABOUT THAT EVENING.
I HAD TO CALL THOMAS AT WORK TO PICK UP THE GROCERIES ON HIS WAY HOME, SO I DIDN'T HAVE DINNER READY.
DID THOMAS SEEM ANGRY?
AT... AT FIRST. BUT NOT BECAUSE OF THAT.
PLEASE, THOMAS, PLEASE. TAKE ROSLIN TO THE DOCTOR. I CAN'T TAKE THIS ANY MORE.
I'M AFRAID OF WHAT I MIGHT DO.

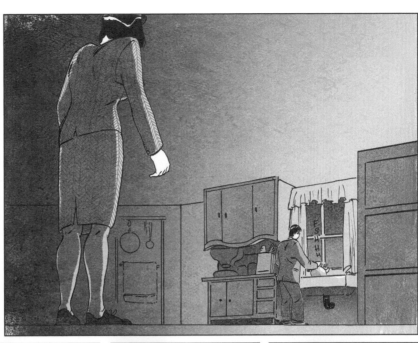

I THINK I'll HAVE SOME TEA UNTIL DINNER IS READY.

FWUP

HHH

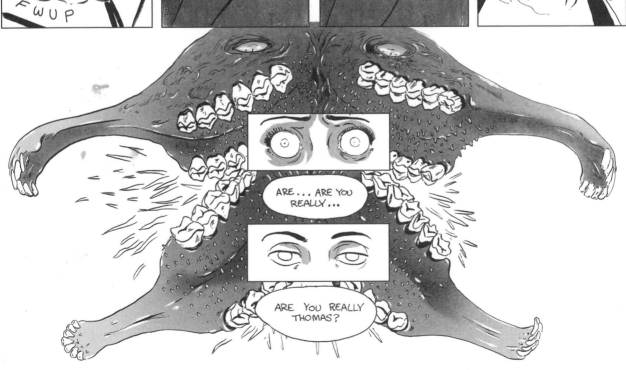

ARE... ARE YOU REALLY...

ARE YOU REALLY THOMAS?

THAT MUST HAVE BEEN VERY FRIGHTENING.

IT WAS ONLY FOR A MOMENT, I CAN'T EVEN SAY *WHAT* I SAW, ONLY THAT ...THAT I AM *CERTAIN*, NOW, TRULY CERTAIN, THAT THE MAN WHO CAME DOWN THE ATTIC STAIRS ISN'T THOMAS.

WHAT DO YOU INTEND TO DO, EMMA?

I'll... I'll STAY WITH MY MOTHER.

AND WHAT ABOUT ROSLIN?

I'LL TAKE HER WITH ME, OF COURSE, AND THEN I'LL TAKE MY UNCLE'S CAR TO A DOCTOR SO ROSLIN CAN GET HELP.

EMMA, DO YOU REMEMBER ANYTHING ABOUT ROSLIN'S BIRTH?

WHAT?

NO, I HAD TWILIGHT SLEEP, IT SHOULD SAY SO RIGHT THERE IN MY FILE.

AND YOU NEVER BREASTFED?

NO, I WAS GIVEN A SHOT RIGHT AFTER. DOCTOR, WHAT IS THIS ABOUT?

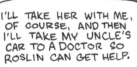

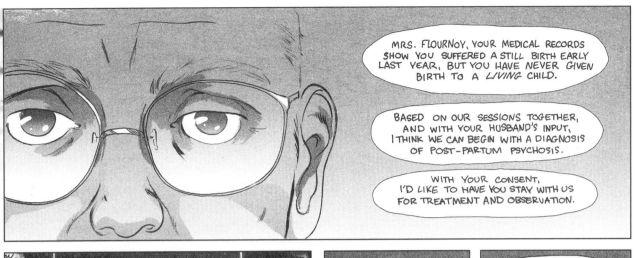

MRS. FLOURNOY, YOUR MEDICAL RECORDS SHOW YOU SUFFERED A STILL BIRTH EARLY LAST YEAR, BUT YOU HAVE NEVER GIVEN BIRTH TO A *LIVING* CHILD.

BASED ON OUR SESSIONS TOGETHER, AND WITH YOUR HUSBAND'S INPUT, I THINK WE CAN BEGIN WITH A DIAGNOSIS OF POST-PARTUM PSYCHOSIS.

WITH YOUR CONSENT, I'D LIKE TO HAVE YOU STAY WITH US FOR TREATMENT AND OBSERVATION.

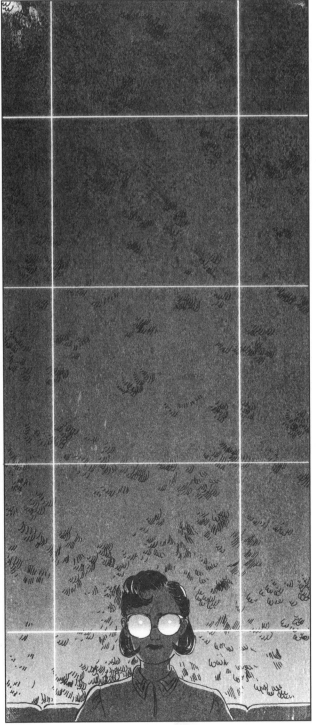

THAT IS CERTAINLY A LOT TO CONSIDER, DR. OEMING.

IF I PROMISE NOT TO DO ANYTHING RASH, MAY I HAVE SOME TIME TO THINK IT OVER?

BY ALL MEANS; I THINK THAT'S VERY REASONABLE OF YOU. YOU HAVE MY NUMBER.

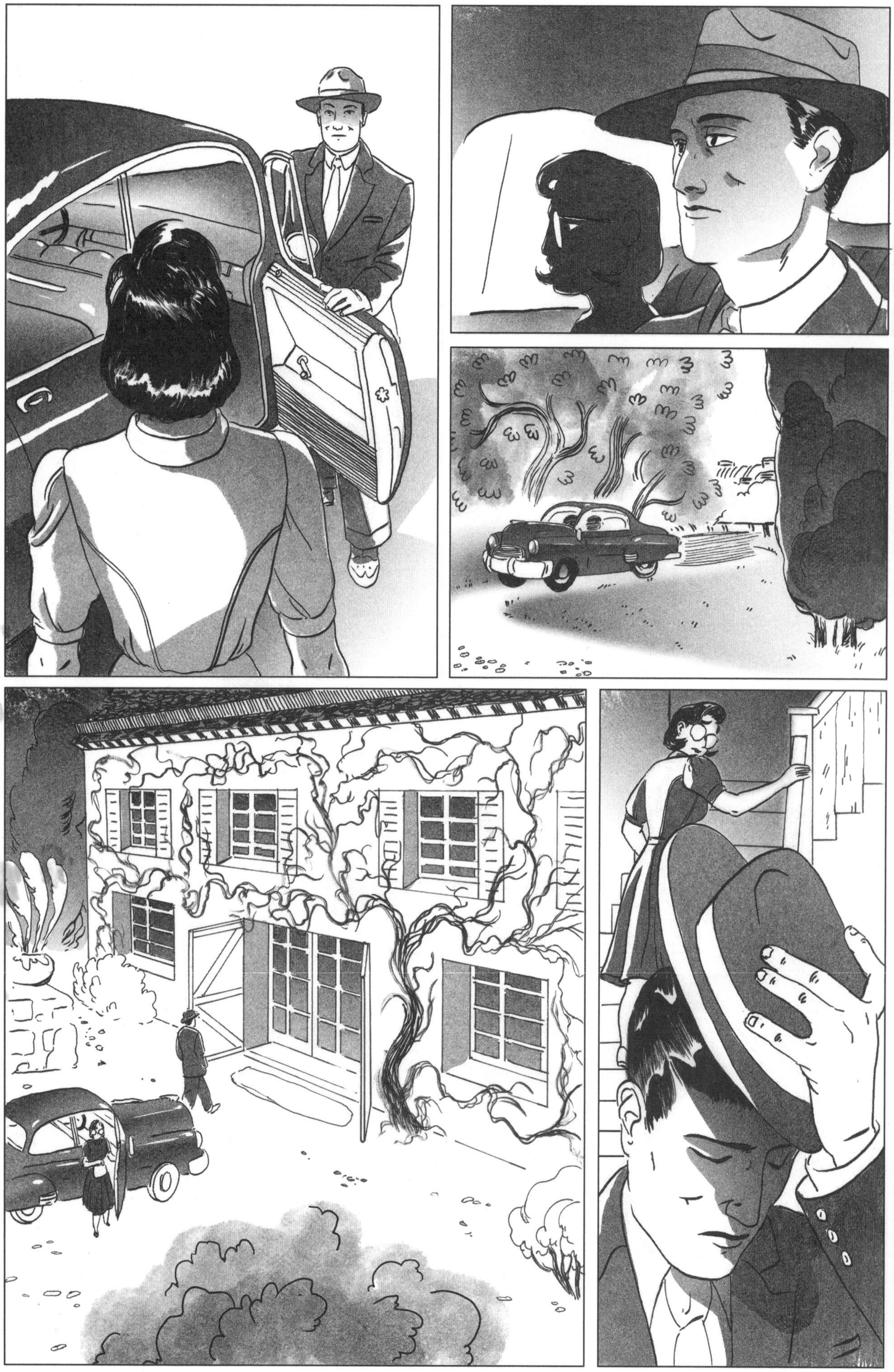

I HAVE ONE CHANCE.

ONE CHANCE TO DO THIS.

I'LL COOK DINNER, AND THEN WHEN THOMAS IS ASLEEP I'LL TAKE THE KEYS AND ROSLIN AND WE'LL BE MILES AWAY BEFORE HE KNOWS I'M GONE.

IT HAS TO BE SOMEONE HE DOESN'T KNOW, SOMEONE I'VE NEVER TOLD HIM ABOUT.

EDITH? NO, HER HUSBAND WOULD CALL THE POLICE.

I WON'T GO TO MY MOTHER'S, THAT'S THE FIRST PLACE HE'LL LOOK.

RUTH, IT COULD BE RUTH, I COULD AT LEAST STOP BY, FIND OUT IF IT'S SAFE.

WAIT.

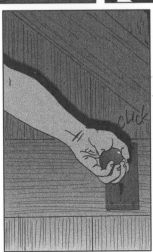

CLICK

IF I'M WRONG...

IF I'M WRONG...

BUT IF I'M RIGHT...

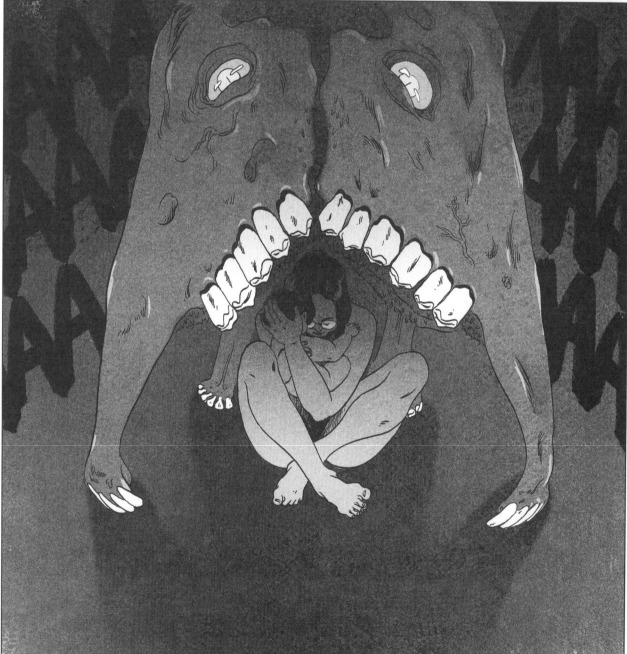

OH, ROSLIN!

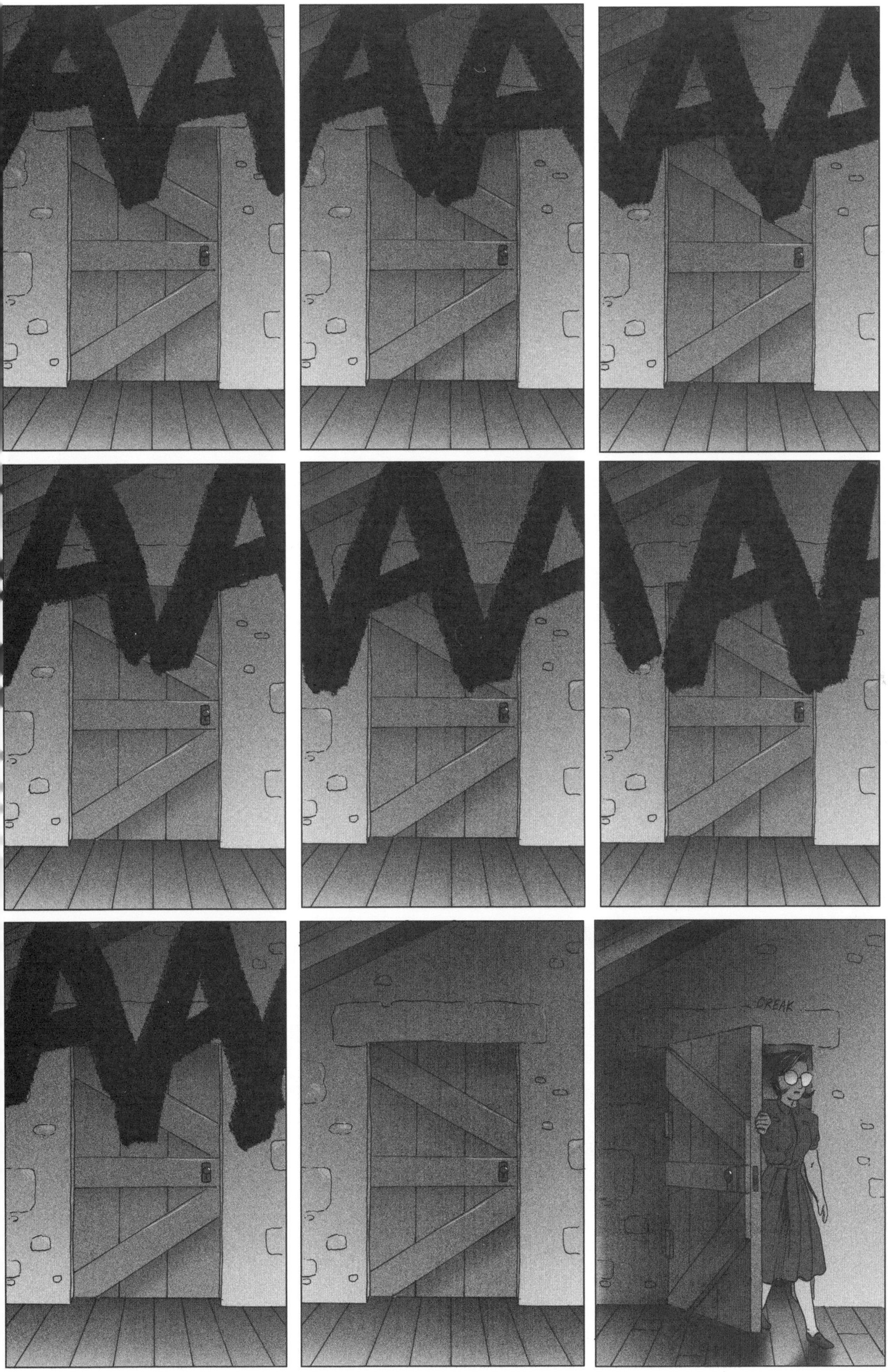
CREAK

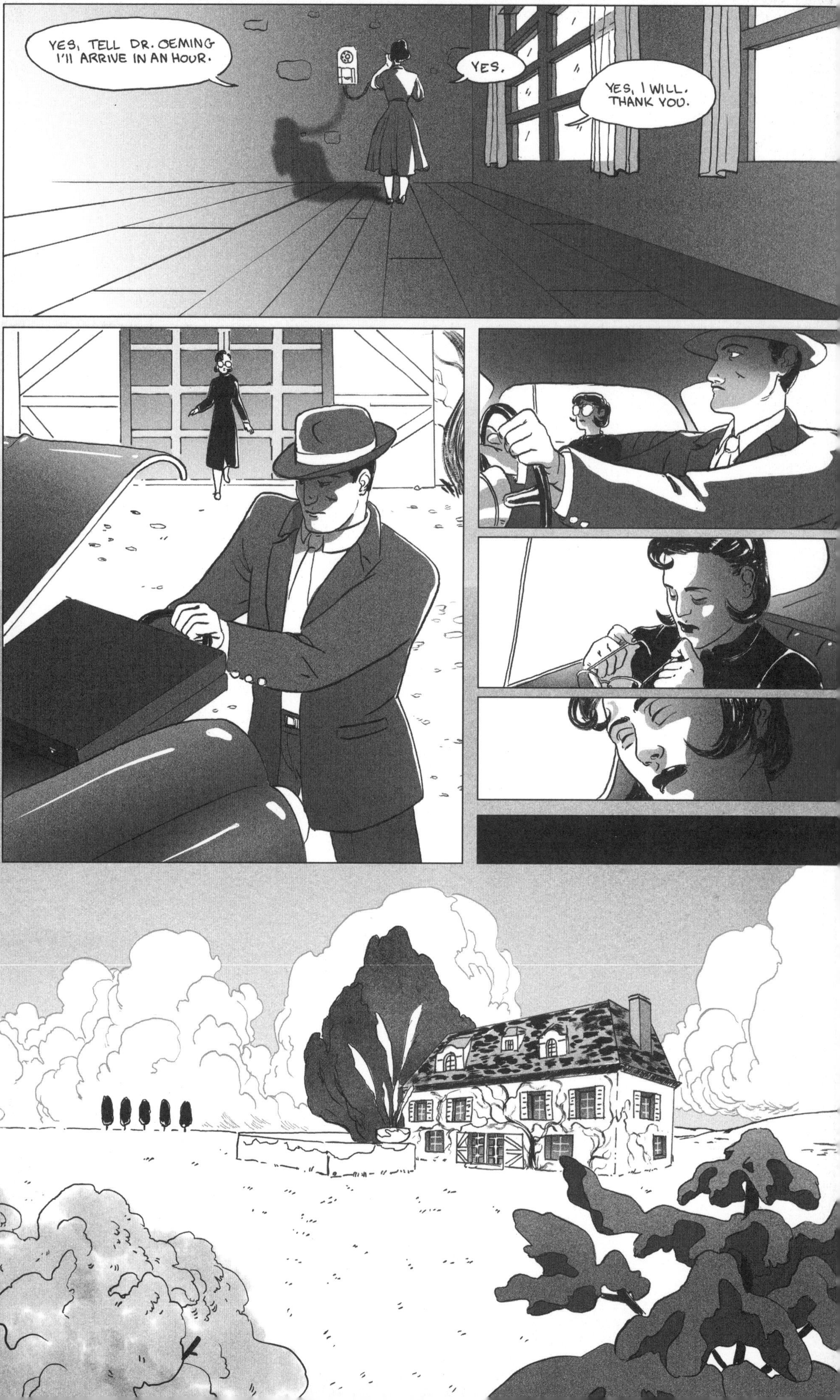
YES, TELL DR. OEMING I'LL ARRIVE IN AN HOUR.
YES.
YES, I WILL. THANK YOU.

Author's Note

Although this book deals with the theme of postpartum depression, it was conceived at a time where I was experiencing very intense emotions about motherhood. I was grappling with an all-consuming urge to start a family, while also suffering from extreme anxiety about motherhood and the possibility of regretting a choice I could never take back. Drawing this story was my way of exploring those fears in a safe way.

While Marilyn French's semi-autobiographical writings documenting the routine of pre-war childcare and housekeeping informed parts of this book, I personally have no lived experience of motherhood and this book is not meant to reflect such.

If you are struggling with postpartum depression, please tell someone. You can find out more information at:

Postpartum Support International
www.postpartum.net

Or call the National Suicide Prevention Hotline:
1-800-273-8255

About the Author

Celine Loup is an illustrator and Ignatz Award-nominated cartoonist who currently lives in France. She has done illustration work for *The New York Times, The New Yorker,* The A.V. Club, *Variety, Lucky Peach,* and Medium. Loup is the acclaimed creator of popular comics such as *Honey* and *Mother,* as well as her current ongoing series, *Hestia.* Her work has garnered an Ignatz Awards nomination, recognition on the Best American Comics "Notable Books" list, and acclaim from American Illustration, The Society of Illustrators, and CMYK.